BRITISH TANKS OF THE RED ARMY

Peter Samsonov

First published in Great Britain in 2024
by Gallantry Books
an imprint of Mortons Books Ltd.
Media Centre
Morton Way
Horncastle LN9 6JR
www.mortonsbooks.co.uk

Copyright © Gallantry Books, 2024

All rights reserved. No part of this publication may be reproduced or transmitted in any form or by any means, electronic or mechanical including photocopying, recording, or any information storage retrieval system without prior permission in writing from the publisher.

ISBN 978-1-911794-06-5

The right of Peter Samsonov to be identified as the author of this work has been asserted in accordance with the Copyright, Designs and Patents Act 1988.

Typeset by Jayne Clements, Hinoki, Design and Typesetting (jayne@hinoki.co.uk)
Printed and bound in Great Britain

Acknowledgements
The author would like to thank Yuri Pasholok, whose research made this work possible, as well as Pierre-Olivier Buan and Pavel Borovikov for providing photographs used in this book.

Contents

Introduction	7
I. British Infantry Tanks in Soviet Service	13
Infantry Tank Mk.II (Matilda)	13
Infantry Tank Mk.III (Valentine)	22
The First Generation: Valentine I, Valentine II, Valentine IV	22
Return of the Three-Man Turret: Valentine III and V	26
Canadian Valentines: Valentine VI, VII, and VIIA	28
Firepower Upgrade: Valentine IX and X	36
Soviet Upgrades	40
Infantry Tank Mk.IV (Churchill)	45
Churchill I-IV	45
Churchill Crocodile	53
Battle of Stalingrad	55
Battle of Kursk	58
Leningrad and Pskov Offensives	62
II. Matilda and Valentine Tanks in Combat	67
Battle of Moscow	68
Second Battle of Kharkov	75
Battle of Voronezh	80
Battle of the Caucasus	84
Battle of Kursk	90
Operation Bagration	96
III. British Light Tanks and Cruisers in the USSR	102
Light Tank Mk.VII (Tetrarch)	103
Cruiser Tanks Mk.IV and Mk.VI	108
Cruiser Tank Mk.VIII (Cromwell)	111
IV. Conclusions	118
Profiles	120
Glossary	124
Endnotes	126
Index	134

Introduction

THE FIRST encounter between British armour and the Red Army was not on friendly terms. After the conclusion of the First World War, the British sent a number of surplus tanks to reinforce the pro-monarchy White Army in the Russian Civil War. These tanks failed to tip the scales in the Whites' favour.

In addition to the difficulty of operating early unreliable machines, White officers had no experience in coordinating combined arms warfare and could not use these vehicles effectively in battle. Furthermore, while the battlefields of the Western Front were characterised by mud, trenches, barbed wire, and slow grind through enemy defences, the Russian Civil War was a war of manoeuvre. Success was dictated by mobile cavalry forces and armoured trains. Early tanks that could barely move faster than walking pace found themselves out of their element.

The Worker and Peasant Red Army (RKKA) was victorious in the Russian Civil War. Operating on a shoestring budget with little heavy industry to rely on, Red commanders were forced to make the most of what they had, including war trophies. The rhomboid Mark V heavy tanks entered service with the RKKA under the name 'Ricardo', after the brand of the engine. Medium Tanks Mk.A (Whippet) and Mk.B (Hornet) were also put to work but all of these types were found wanting.

Out of all the captured tanks, only the French Renault FT was deemed satisfactory. The vehicle served as a prototype for a vehicle designated 'Russian Renault'. This was a little more than a copy with only minor adaptations designed to make it easier to produce in Soviet factories, but it was a start.[1] Soviet tank building grew out of this French influence. The T-16 small infantry support tank built in 1927 was visually reminiscent of the Renault FT and contemporary French designs, although the tanks had very little in common from a technical standpoint.[2]

The boost given by this French 'inheritance' had run its course by the end of the 1920s.

Vickers-Carden-Loyd M1931 tank, Patriot Park. While it was not copied entirely, it served as a starting point for the Soviet T-37A amphibious tank. PAVEL BOROVIKOV

The T-18 (successor to the T-16) was built in great numbers, but the army's appetite began to outgrow its limitations. These tanks were used in battle during the conflict for the Eastern Chinese Railway in 1929 and had a tremendous effect on Chinese warlords, but Red Army officers supervising their deployment were unsatisfied. A long laundry list of updated requirements was sent to Moscow, with the commanders' demands chiefly focused around the need for greater mobility.[3] This requirement proved difficult to meet.

Development of the T-19 and T-20 tanks proceeded slowly, and it seemed unlikely that these tanks would be mobile enough.[4] Work on the T-24 manoeuvre tank and T-17 tankette was also going nowhere. The RKKA's armoured doctrine and its desire for improved hardware outpaced the ability of industry to provide suitable vehicles.[5]

The solution was once again to seek inspiration abroad. A commission from the Directorate of Mechanisation and Motorisation (UMM) was sent to France, the United Kingdom and the United States of America to obtain samples of vehicles. The scale of the purchase was truly massive, as the USSR was looking not to just buy a handful of tanks, but also to acquire a licence for mass production and assistance from foreign industry experts—both in designing tanks and in assembling the factories that would build them.

At one stage it seemed possible that the development of Soviet armour might continue to follow in step with the French, as the Renault NC-27 infantry tank was on the shopping list.

Yet for better or for worse, this deal

T-38 amphibious tank, Museum of National Military History. This tank was a further evolution of the T-37A design. There is an undeniable family resemblance to the Vickers tank pictured opposite. PAVEL BOROVIKOV

did not go through. Instead, the Soviets found British armour to be much more promising, particularly the designs of Vickers-Armstrongs and Carden-Loyd. The USSR was one of many nations to take an interest in the Carden-Loyd Mk.VI tankette. This vehicle was produced in the USSR under the designation T-27.[6] The Soviet tank commission also noticed the Vickers-Carden-Loyd M1931 tank. A sample was purchased and led to the development of the T-37A amphibious tank.[7]

The Vickers Mk.E Type A or Vickers 6-tonner was another popular product that the UMM did not overlook. Trials in the USSR showed that while the armament of two machine guns was not satisfactory (the T-18 was armed with one machine gun and one 37mm cannon), the chassis showed great promise. A licensed copy of the Vickers Mk.E entered production in 1931 under the name T-26. A short 37mm gun replaced one of the machine guns to make up the shortfall in firepower, and a large two-man turret with a long 45mm gun was introduced in 1933. The T-26 became the most common Soviet tank in the interbellum RKKA.[8]

The commission also purchased a number of Vickers 12-tonners (Medium Tank Mk.II), but this was a bust. These tanks were not as promising as their lighter cousins and no copy was put into mass production.

Vickers Mk.E Type B tank, Bovington Tank Museum. The twin-turreted variant of this tank served as the starting point in the development of the T-26, the most common Soviet tank of the 1930s.

They were eventually stripped of their engines and running gear in order to be installed as armoured machine gun nests along the western border of the USSR, but photographs taken by German troops in the summer of 1941 suggest that most if not all 12-tonners remained rusting above ground.[9]

The Vickers 16-tonner (Medium Tank Mk.III) was also of interest to the Soviet commission. This tank was not purchased, but the T-28 prototype designed some time after the commission's return had a similar layout. Unlike the T-26 and T-27, the T-28 was not a copy of the British design, as the UMM did not have the opportunity to study the vehicle closely. In the end, the tank turned out to be a mix of original Soviet ideas and solutions inspired by components of the Grosstraktor tank that was tested in secret at the proving grounds at Kazan.[10] While a resemblance can be seen between the British five-turreted A1E1 Independent and Soviet T-35 tanks, there is no evidence that the commission took any interest in it. Even British specialists who had a chance to see T-28 and T-35 tanks in 1941 drew a parallel with the Vickers 16-tonner rather than the Independent.[11]

As with the relics of the First World War, the British-inspired tanks had no offspring. As the USSR became capable of producing light tanks in sufficient quantities, a tankette was no longer needed. The successors to

INTRODUCTION

T-26 tank, Vadim Zadorozhniy Technical Museum. The T-26 started as a copy of the Vickers Mk.E Type A adapted for Soviet production, but evolved into a very different tank by the mid-1930s, including a completely original turret. PAVEL BOROVIKOV

the T-26 also had little to do with the original British tank. The T-46 developed in the mid-1930s was more reminiscent of Christie's tanks with its large road wheels and convertible drive.[12] The T-28 was replaced by the KV-1 heavy tank, also an entirely original vehicle.[13] The T-37A and T-38 were replaced by the T-40 small amphibious tank, which had nothing in common with its ancestors.[14]

The new generation of tanks was slow to overtake the old one. People's Commissar of Defence Marshal K. Ye. Voroshilov estimated that the rapidly expanding Red Army's need for armour would be met by 1943, at which point the old types of tanks could finally be phased out completely. However, those plans were thrown into chaos in the summer of 1941. Tremendous losses of armoured vehicles in the first months of the war with Germany required the Red Army to once again look abroad to resupply its tank forces.[15]

The British themselves were facing a tank production crisis. The defeat of the British Expeditionary Force in 1940 resulted in the abandonment of some 691 modern tanks on the continent.[16] With a followup invasion of the Home Islands seemingly the next logical step, the regular army and Home Guard scrambled for any form of armoured vehicle, either traditionally designed or cobbled together by well-meaning volunteers, no matter how outdated or ineffective.[17]

Great Britain was in a much stronger position by the summer of 1941. Both the quality and quantity of British armoured vehicles had improved. The Infantry Tank Mk.II (Matilda) that had already proved itself a formidable opponent to tanks of the Axis in France and North Africa was joined by the Infantry Tank Mk.III (Valentine) and Infantry Tank Mk.IV (Churchill). The obsolete Light Tank Mk.VI was replaced with new high-speed tanks: Light Tank Mk.VII (Tetrarch), Cruiser Tanks Mk.V (Covenanter) and Mk.VI (Crusader).

An invasion across the Channel also seemed considerably less likely than it did a year prior, especially since the German campaign against the USSR was not going as well as Hitler hoped. Rather than a swift blow that would cause the Soviet state to crumble, the Germans were now involved in a lengthy and costly war. The British could now do their part to prolong it, confident that equipment sent to the USSR would not end up in German hands shortly after its delivery.

Work to provide large-scale military aid to the USSR began in August 1941, culminating with the 1st Moscow Conference (also known as the Three Power Conference) on October 1, 1941. Even though this assistance is colloquially lumped under the term 'lend lease', the ability to "sell, transfer title to, exchange, lease, lend, or otherwise dispose of" military hardware granted by the Act to Promote the Defense of the United States (commonly known as the Lend Lease Act) only applied to American supplies.

The British offered help under a separate programme and this help did not come for free. Although Great Britain offered a credit of £10 million, the USSR was paying in natural resources. Some deliveries were expected months after the Three Power Conference had concluded, while others were required urgently: up to 1,000 tons of pine tar, 10,000 tons of chrome ore, 1,400kg of platinum (with a note that 700kg was to be sent immediately), as well as 250,000 rifles with 1,000 rounds of ammunition for each.[18]

Supplies of tanks began even before the conference took place. Convoy PQ-1 with the first 20 British tanks for the Red Army left for Arkhangelsk on September 29. These tanks arrived in time to take place in the Battle of Moscow. British armoured vehicles would remain in service with the Red Army until the conclusion of the Second World War nearly four years later.[19]

I.
British Infantry Tanks in Soviet Service

Infantry Tank Mk.II (Matilda)

The British army began to modernise its armoured vehicles in 1934, after a five-year lull. This modernisation was both evolutionary and revolutionary. In part, the old class of medium tanks was done away with, replaced by fast but relatively lightly armoured Cruiser tanks and slow but thick-skinned Infantry tanks. At the same time, the existing concepts were not abandoned entirely. Experience gained by the Woolwich Arsenal in building the Medium Tank A6 and the unsuccessful Medium Tank A7 came in handy when building the new generation of tanks.[20]

A tank with the General Staff specification number A12 began to take shape in 1936. The most impressive aspect of the design was the unparalleled thickness of its armour; the new tank was protected by up to 75mm of steel. Casting was used extensively in order to speed up production. The armament consisted of the same 40mm 2-pounder gun and coaxial machine gun used by other British tanks of that generation. The tank's power plant consisted of two 8.75 L AEC A183/A184 bus engines, a solution taken from the Medium Tank A7E3. The Wilson planetary gearbox and elements of the suspension and running gear were also taken from this tank. The A12 was not just an upgraded A7E3, as major elements such as the turret were designed entirely from scratch. A prototype indexed A12E1 entered trials on April 11, 1938, joined by the improved A12E2 on

Infantry Tank Mk.IIA or Matilda II, Base Borden. This tank had a BESA coaxial machine gun, unlike the Vickers machine gun on the original Infantry Tank Mk.II.

December 15.[21] Despite the successful trials and decision to put it into production as the Infantry Tank Mk.II, the design continued to evolve. Following the adoption of the BESA machine gun into service in 1939, it was installed in the new infantry tank starting in 1940. These tanks received a new index: Infantry Tank Mk.IIA. The AEC engines were replaced with a pair of 6.8L 95hp Leyland E148/E149 engines in the spring of 1941. Tanks with the new engine were called Infantry Tank Mk.IIA*. As the British transitioned to using easier to remember names, the Infantry Tank Mk.II received the designation Matilda I, the Mk.IIA became the Matilda II, and the Mk.IIA* became Matilda III. The Matilda III CS was also put into production in the summer of 1941. Like other British close support tanks, this tank had a 3in howitzer instead of a 2-pounder gun. This weapon was designed to primarily fire smoke shells, but could fire HE as well.[22]

The next variant of the Matilda went into production in the fall of 1941. The Leyland engines were replaced yet again, this time with the E170/E171. The tank had a visually distinguishing feature: the commander's cupola was much lower than that of its predecessors. This was the most common variant of the Matilda, making up 60% of the tanks of this type. The fifth and final variant of the Matilda was equipped with

Infantry Tank Mk.IIA or Matilda III, Saumur tank museum. The Matilda III had a pair of Leyland engines instead of the AEC engines used on the Infantry Tanks Mk.II and Mk.IIA.*

a Westinghouse servo mechanism to make driving the tank easier.

The contract for these tanks was given to Harland & Wolff in March 1942 and the last tank was delivered in August 1943. The British became disillusioned with the Matilda long before that. The tank couldn't take a weapon larger than the 2-pounder, which was rapidly becoming obsolete. The reliability of the Matilda also left much to be desired, and its low speed made it a poor candidate for the long-range armoured thrusts that became characteristic of the North African theatre of war. Because of this, most Matilda IV and V tanks were sent to Australia and the USSR rather than serving with the British Army.[23]

The USSR first learned about the Matilda in September 1941. A hastily composed intelligence report dated September 17 described a 32-ton "medium tank model 1940" with 70mm of armour and a 300hp engine, armed with a 47mm gun and one machine gun. The data was quickly corrected. Three days later, the GABTU was informed that "British mark 2 tanks" were already on their way to Arkhangelsk. More detailed data arrived on the next day, although there were still some errors. This was the first report to use the name Matilda, although Soviet documents continued to refer to the tank as MK-II or MK-2 for the duration of the war.[24]

Matilda IV CS, Patriot Park. The Matilda IV had a lower, less vulnerable commander's cupola than the Matilda III. The CS (Close Support) variant carried a 76mm howitzer that could fire HE or smoke shells. PAVEL BOROVIKOV

Shipments began to trickle in starting in October 1941. Convoys PQ-1 and PQ-2 delivered 49 Matildas by October 30. PQ-2 also carried a team of British instructors to train Soviet tankers. Convoy PQ-3 arrived in Arkhangelsk on November 22 with 70 Matilda III tanks and 145 Matilda tanks had been delivered by the end of the year. The poor condition of the tanks on arrival delayed their combat debut. Tanks were packed badly and often with incomplete equipment, as a result of which they were damaged in transit and could not be repaired on arrival. The rates of damage were high: on December 2, 1941, the Gorky Automotive and Armour Centre reported that 58 out of the 137 tanks inspected so far arrived broken. A torrent of correspondence erupted between Soviet and British officials and the quality of shipments slowly improved over time. The low reliability of the Matildas became a serious problem, as many tanks broke down even in training conditions.[25]

A bigger issue had to do with the tank's armament. Matildas arrived with just five to six loads of ammunition. As a result, tanks quickly ran out of ammo and became useless. Tanks with damaged guns also could not be repaired, as no spare barrels were supplied. The issue was resolved quickly however, as Convoys PQ-6 and PQ-7 carried large quantities of ammunition. The British dispatched 750 HE and 250 smoke rounds with each Matilda CS and 617 rounds with AP shot for regular Matildas going forward.[26]

The story with ammunition shortages had an interesting consequence. Even while ammunition was available, Soviet tankers didn't like the fact that the Matilda's 2-pounder gun only fired solid shot and did not have any HE shells or even AP shells with HE filler. The 2-pounder gun itself was considered too weak; the Matilda had the mass of a medium tank and the armour of a heavy one, but its armament was more suitable for a light tank.

These problems could all be solved in one fell swoop by replacing the gun with a domestic weapon. Unlike the British, who gave up on installing anything larger than a 2-pounder into the Matilda's turret, the Soviets decided to put in a gun more befitting the Matilda's weight class. The 76mm ZIS-5 gun used on the KV-1 tank was chosen for installation. The variant developed for the Matilda at factory #92 was designated F-96. The F-96 gun mount also carried a DT machine gun, which meant that the new tank would not be dependent on British ammunition supplies. New ammunition racks were developed along with the new gun and the tank carried a total of 54 rounds for the 76mm gun; quite a feat, considering that the regular Matilda only carried 69 of the much smaller 2-pounder shells.

A Matilda III tank with WD number T.10157 was chosen for the initial conversion. The work finished quickly and trials were held between December 2 and 11, 1941. The new gun mount worked well; it took no more than 6kg of effort to elevate the gun and 5kg to traverse the turret, although due to the offset balance it required 30kg of effort to turn the turret if the tank was tilted by 6°. This problem could be solved by a counterweight on the back of the turret. The large gun mantlet clipped the cooling grilles if the turret was traversed backwards, but this problem could be solved on production tanks by trimming the grilles and changing the shape on the mantlet.

No defects were discovered during the trials, although the narrow 1,370mm turret ring made working with the gun difficult; it could only be depressed to -2°. Nevertheless, the project was approved. The proving grounds recommended that production should begin once minor design defects were corrected and conversion of the necessary components could be performed at factory #112 (Krasnoye Sormovo). The prototype was shown to the Soviet government in January 1942 and a proposal for conversion of 120 tanks was drafted.

Unfortunately, the conversion scheme had a powerful opponent: GABTU Chief Lieutenant General Fedorenko spoke out against this idea. In his opinion, the turret was cramped and uncomfortable when such a large gun was installed. Additionally, the aforementioned problems with ammunition shipments had already been resolved. Fedorenko considered it to be more sensible to set up domestic production of 2-pounder ammunition if supplies ran dry again. This would be easier than converting British tanks. Furthermore, factory #112 was busy building the T-34, which was a much more useful vehicle than a Matilda, regardless of what gun it was equipped with. Reducing T-34 production was considered unacceptable when the situation on the front lines was so unstable. The Red Army decided to abandon the conversion project.[27]

A delay associated with the evacuation of the NIBT Proving Grounds from Kubinka to Kazan meant that trials of an ordinary Matilda tank were conducted after trials of

The Matilda's tracks were designed to perform in mud, but worked poorly on ice and snow. This photo shows remnants of an ice cleat welded onto one of the track links. Soviet tankers developed several improvised methods to improve performance of foreign tanks in winter. PAVEL BOROVIKOV

the experimental one. A Matilda III tank with WD number T.6886 built by Vulcan was chosen. This tank had been among the first Matildas to reach the USSR.

Since the 2-pounder gun and radio were already tested on a Valentine II, the Matilda went through an abbreviated testing programme. In addition to a study of the tank's technical features, the Matilda was to be driven on a 1,000km long course, 300km of which was on a highway. This plan was not followed precisely since the Matilda was only driven 95km off-road and 813km on a cobblestone road. The quality of the road limited the tank's top speed to just 21.1kph and it took an average of 25 seconds to reach this speed. Average speed on this road was just 14.5kph and the tank burned 169 litres of fuel per 100km of driving. Off-road, the tank's average speed dropped to just 7.7kph and fuel consumption spiked to 396 litres per 100km.

The Matilda was clearly designed for much warmer climates, which affected its performance in winter. Traction in snow and on ice was poor, limiting the tank to slopes no steeper than 12° in winter conditions. Traction could be improved by welding spurs onto the tracks. This improved grip and reduced the turning radius from 10-13m to just 4-5m, but the spurs wore down quickly when driving on hard surfaces.

One of the weakest points in the tank was its engine. The Leyland engines had a

Engine deck of a Matilda II tank, Base Borden. None of the engines installed in this tank produced enough power to give the 25-ton Matilda good mobility.

combined weight of 1,000kg but put out just 180hp, compared to 500hp produced by the 750kg V-2 engine mounted in a T-34 tank. This weak engine severely limited the Matilda's mobility in snow. The tank could drive through snow banks up to 600mm deep, but artificial obstacles were much more difficult to negotiate. A Matilda tank tested against a series of packed snow walls in January 1942 took 21 minutes and multiple tries to overcome its obstacles. To compare, a Valentine tank took 14 minutes to overcome the same walls and a T-34 punched through in just ten seconds.

While Soviet testers judged the engine very harshly, there were plenty of positive aspects to this tank. The minimal number of access ports and hatches preserved the protection granted by the thick armour. The tank's suspension was protected as well. Observation from the tank was quite good thanks to the range of vision provided by Mk.IV periscopes. The Wilson planetary gearbox was also quite interesting. An experimental gearbox inspired by this design was developed for the KV-1, although it was never built.

Overall, opinions formed during the tank's proving ground trials were mixed. It had thick armour going for it, but nothing else. The gun was incapable of engaging the

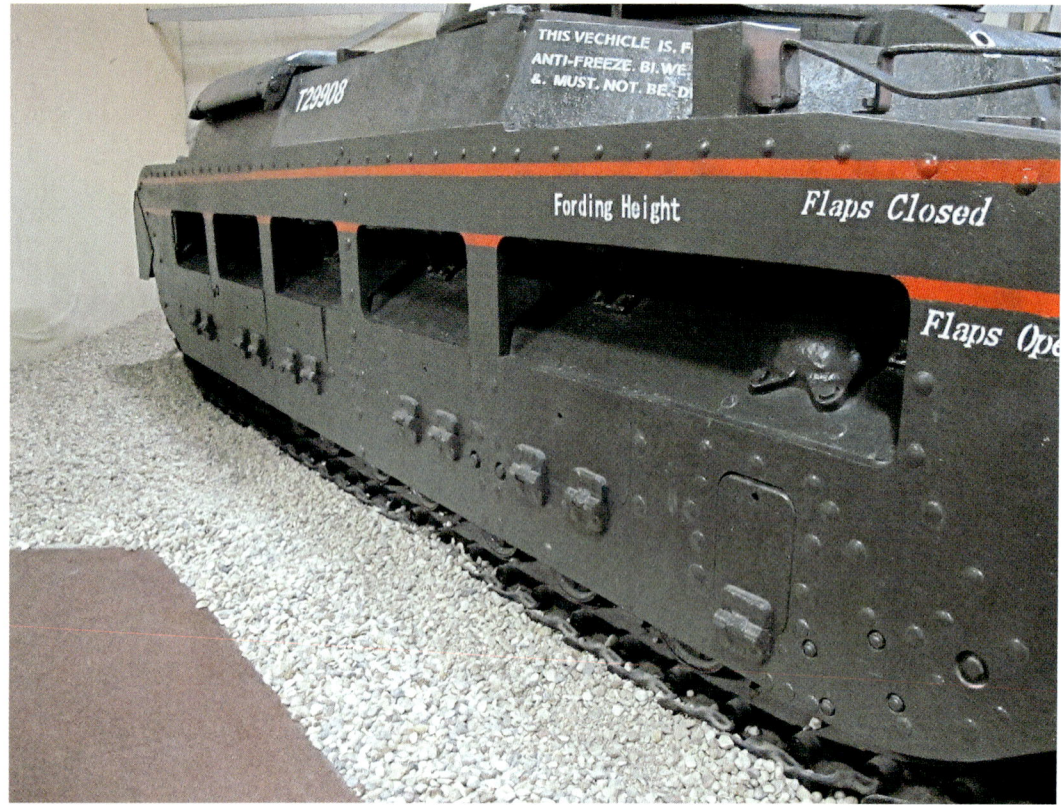
Spaced armour protected the side of the tank, but also made access to the running gear difficult.

latest German medium tanks from the front. The low engine power and low fuel capacity severely limited both mobility and range.[28]

Nevertheless, shipments of Matilda tanks continued. 129 arrived in January 1942, 47 in February, and 170 in March. This was the largest delivery of Matildas for the entire war. Only 40 tanks were delivered in April, 21 in May, and 73 in June. Deliveries cratered with the destruction of Convoy PQ-17; only six tanks arrived in July and none in August. Shipments jumped back up to 84 in September, but would never again reach their former peak. None arrived in October and December with 56 more tanks arriving in November for a total of 771 Matilda tanks delivered in 1942.[29]

In 1942, Soviet planners decided to cease ordering Matilda tanks upon the conclusion of the current contract. Preference was given to Matildas with 76 mm howitzers, as the 40 mm 2-pounder was looking fairly anaemic by 1942.[30]

There was a small burst of deliveries in early 1943, with 10 tanks delivered in January, 54 in February, and 81 in March. With this, shipments of the Matilda tank to the USSR ended. 1,084 Matilda tanks of all types were sent to the USSR between September 1941 and March 1943, although only 916 arrived at their destination. All Matilda tanks that did arrive in the USSR were shipped via the Arctic convoys.[31]

Even though these tanks were

Matilda IV CS tank, Victory Museum at Poklonnaya Gora. The turret is a modern replica and only the hull is original. It is possible that the original turret was discarded after the tank was converted into a prime mover. PAVEL BOROVIKOV

unsatisfactory by 1943, they continued to serve in the Red Army. It had 315 tanks of this type in active service by January 1944 and 201 were still in service by June 1. Matilda tanks were gradually pulled back from the front lines, although they were still used in battle. Ten Matildas were lost in action between January 1 and May 9, 1945.[32]

By May 23, 1945, 222 Matilda tanks settled in the Far Eastern military districts. Only 45 were functional and 177 needed refurbishment.[33] Worn out tanks were of little use, as spare parts for Matildas were no longer being imported.[34] Eight Matildas were ordered to be scrapped in 1947 with an undisclosed number sold to the agricultural sector at scrap value.[35]

Since the combat history of the Matilda tank in the Red Army is closely intertwined with that of the Valentine, both will be covered in a separate chapter.

Infantry Tank Mk.III (Valentine)

The First Generation: Valentine I, Valentine II, Valentine IV

Leslie Francis Little, Vickers' chief tank designer, began working on what he considered to be the ideal infantry tank in 1937. This tank was a successor to the Infantry Tank Mk.I and Cruiser Tank Mk.II. The general shape of the hull came from the former and the suspension came from the latter. This tank weighed 16 tons, much less than the 25-ton Infantry Tank Mk.II.

Little's tank was presented to the War Ministry on February 10, 1938. Since there was no General Staff requirement for a 16-ton infantry tank, the ministry wanted to upgrade his tank to meet the requirements for the A12, with 75mm of armour, a 2-pounder gun, three men in the turret, and a commander's cupola. A compromise was reached: Little incorporated the 2-pounder into the design and increased the armour to 60mm. A Gundlach periscope was added instead of a commander's cupola. The requirement for a third crewman was ignored. This was not good enough for the British army and the project could very well have

An Infantry Tank Mk.III* or Valentine II, Bovington Tank Museum. This tank was completed as a part of the first contract for Valentine tanks awarded to Elswick Works.

BRITISH INFANTRY TANKS IN SOVIET SERVICE

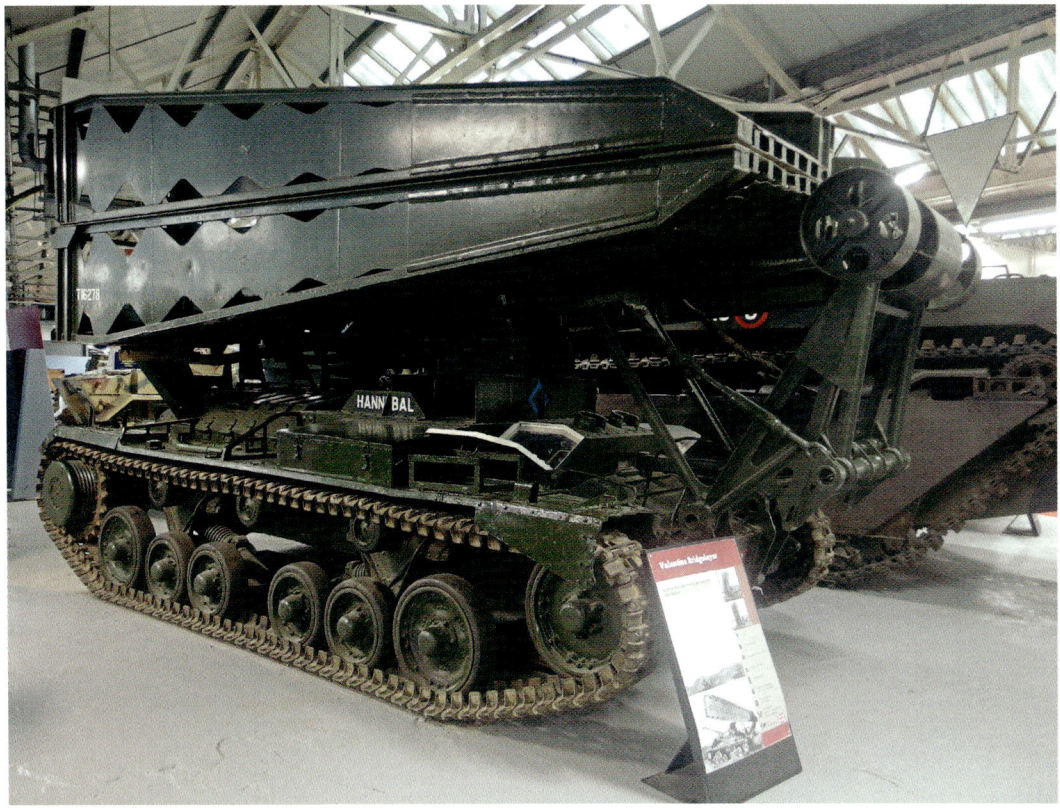

Valentine Bridgelayer built from a Valentine I tank, Bovington Tank Museum. The Valentine I had an AEC A189 gasoline engine, which was replaced with an AEC A190 diesel on the Valentine II.

died here, but the military went back to the bargaining table in April 1939. They backed down on the requirement for a three man turret and unsuccessfully tried to pitch armour to protect the suspension, similar to what was used on the Infantry Tank Mk.II. Little stood his ground, resisting any alterations that would add weight to his tank.[36]

Little's gamble paid off and contracts to produce the Infantry Tank Mk.III were signed with the Metropolitan Cammell Carriage and Wagon Company (MCCW), Birmingham Railway Carriage and Wagon Company (BRC&W), and Elswick Works. Like the Infantry Tank Mk.II, the Mk.III soon changed its engines. The AEC A189 9.64L 131hp gasoline engine was swapped for the more reliable AEC A190 diesel. The tank with the new engine was named Infantry Tank Mk.III*. The Wireless Set No.19 was also introduced to replace the Wireless Set No.11. This radio had a much simpler antenna, positioned on the roof of the turret. 1,493 Infantry Tanks Mk.III* were built[37] but only 161 were sent to the USSR.[38]

Thankfully, the Infantry Tank Mk.III received a proper name before its index had a chance to grow more letters and asterisks. The base model was named Valentine I and the version with an AEC A190 engine was named Valentine II. Another tank soon joined the fray: the Valentine IV had a

Valentine IV tank, Patriot Park. In order to satisfy increased demand for Valentine tanks, the Valentine IV was built with the American GM 6004 diesel engine. PAVEL BOROVIKOV

third type of engine: the American General Motors 6004.[39] This 6.98L 138hp diesel engine was available in sufficient numbers to meet the requirements of growing British tank production. In addition to a new engine, these tanks also had the five-speed synchronised Spicer gearbox, which made them easier to drive than their predecessors. 660 Valentine IV tanks were built, 520 of which were sent to the USSR.[40]

The first Valentine tanks arrived in the USSR with convoy PQ-1. Convoy PQ-2 brought instructors to teach crews and organise repair workshops. Training of Soviet crews began on October 15, 1941 and 120 crews were trained by mid-November. As with the Matilda, the shipping process left much to be desired. The cooling system was filled with water, which froze and expanded during transport through the Arctic, causing pipes and hoses to burst. Tanks stowed on deck with no protection from sea water were severely rusted on arrival. Tanks arrived without spare parts and often even without a complete set of tools and equipment. Furthermore, even though Valentine II tanks were shipped, they arrived with the manual from the Valentine I.

Other issues were discovered after the tanks' arrival. One of the biggest drawbacks discovered during training was the rapid wear of running gear. Each tank came with only three spare track pins, while a week's worth of driving resulted in four to eight replacements. British instructors insisted on tightly stretched tracks, even though it was found that slackening them reduced wear on the track pins. Rubber tyres often broke off the wheels, although this issue did not immobilise the tank.

The same tank from the rear, showing the bulge on the back of the turret that contained a ventilation opening. Air could also pass through the overlapping slats that covered the transmission and engine compartments. This system worked too well in winter and needed to be partially covered up to keep the engine warm enough to run. PAVEL BOROVIKOV

A Valentine II tank with WD number T.17482 was chosen for detailed trials. The tank arrived at the NIBT Proving Grounds in Kazan in December 1941. A lengthy report on the general design of the tank, its components, and crew working conditions was composed there. Soviet testers found the crew compartment cramped and only suitable for crewmen of a medium height. This was particularly crucial for the driver, as his seat position could not be adjusted forwards or backwards. Otherwise, the driver's position was well laid out. The instruments were easy to read. It took 35kg of force to operate the final drive clutches, 65kg to operate the brake pedal, 70kg to operate the clutch, and 1.5kg to operate the gas. This degree of effort was considered acceptable.[41]

The gunner's and loader's stations were also considered well laid out. The 2-pounder gun was aimed with a shoulder stock rather than a flywheel, which was still considered comfortable. When analysing the turret, the Soviet specialists assumed that the gunner doubled as the commander, which was the case in Soviet practice. In British practice, it was the loader who commanded the tank. The large hatch in the roof was a comfortable way to enter and exit the tank. The large ventilation openings cleared the air well if the engine was running, as it sucked air in from the fighting compartment. This was bad news for the crew in winter time, as it meant that they were constantly subjected to a stream of cold air. This introduced another problem in winter: the engine overcooled. This was solved by partially blocking the flow of air with a tarp, plywood, or similar materials.

Mobility trials for this tank were quite lengthy, lasting from December 1941 to March 1942. The tank drove for 1,201km. 971km of this was over a paved road, although the pavement was at times hidden below up to 30cm of snow. Soviet oil was used as British oil was found to be unsatisfactory.

Soviet testers managed to accelerate the tank to 32kph, 8kph above its official top speed. The average driving speed was much lower however, at 14.1kph. The tank chiefly drove in 4th gear. When tackling snow banks 30-70cm deep, the tank drove in 3rd gear, dropping to 2nd for the most difficult segments. The average speed in this condition was 10.4kph. Fuel expenditure was measured at 140L of diesel and 2.2L of oil per 100km of highway or 182L of diesel and 3.7L of oil when driving in snow. The tank lost traction when driving in snow and could not climb a slope steeper than 12° or drive at a tilt of more than 17°.

Trials against man-made snow obstacles also showed that the tank was ill-suited for winter warfare. A 1.7m tall, 4m wide packed-snow wall took 10 attempts to penetrate. An obstacle consisting of two of these walls took 14 minutes to overcome. This was still a better result than the Pz.Kpfw.III Ausf.H, which took 16 minutes. As mentioned previously, the star of this performance was the T-34, which overcame an obstacle made up of three walls in just ten seconds.[42]

Even though the Valentine could not match the mobility of the T-34 tank in difficult conditions, its mobility, armour, and firepower exceeded that of the Soviet T-60 tank.[43] The proving grounds classified it as a medium tank and overall it was judged superior to the Matilda. Opinion of the tank improved as the British reacted to the needs of their new customers: cooling systems filled with ethylene glycol were better suited to the cold and spare parts began arriving in large quantities with convoy PQ-3. Each Valentine tank arrived with 520 rounds of ammunition for its main gun.[44]

Return of the Three-Man Turret: Valentine III and V

Even though the British Army allowed the Valentine tank to go into production with only a two-man turret, they did not give up on a dedicated commander for their tank. This was a considerable challenge, as the 1,270mm wide turret was a tight fit for two, let alone three crewmen. To achieve this without expanding the hull, the front of the turret was stretched out and the gun mount moved forward. Similarly, the turret bustle with the radio was extended backwards. These two changes carved out a little extra room for a commander. The hatch with a two-piece flap stretching across the whole width of the turret was replaced with a circular hatch with a three-piece flap. The front section of the flap contained a Mk.IV periscope, serving as a substitute for a proper commander's cupola. It's hard to call this layout comfortable, but the goal of fitting a third crewman into the turret was achieved.

The larger turret weighed more than the two-man turret, so the sides of the tank had to be thinned out to 50mm to keep the nominal weight to 16 tons. This tank was designated Valentine III. The first contract for 500 tanks numbered T2455 was signed with Birmingham Railway Carriage and Wagon Company on June 26, 1941. BRC&W was the only factory that built Valentine III tanks. 54 tanks from this contract were used to build bridgelayers and 60 chassis were used to build Bishop SPGs. Contract TM6117 for 435 tanks was signed on October 7, 1942. A third contract was signed, but cancelled, and

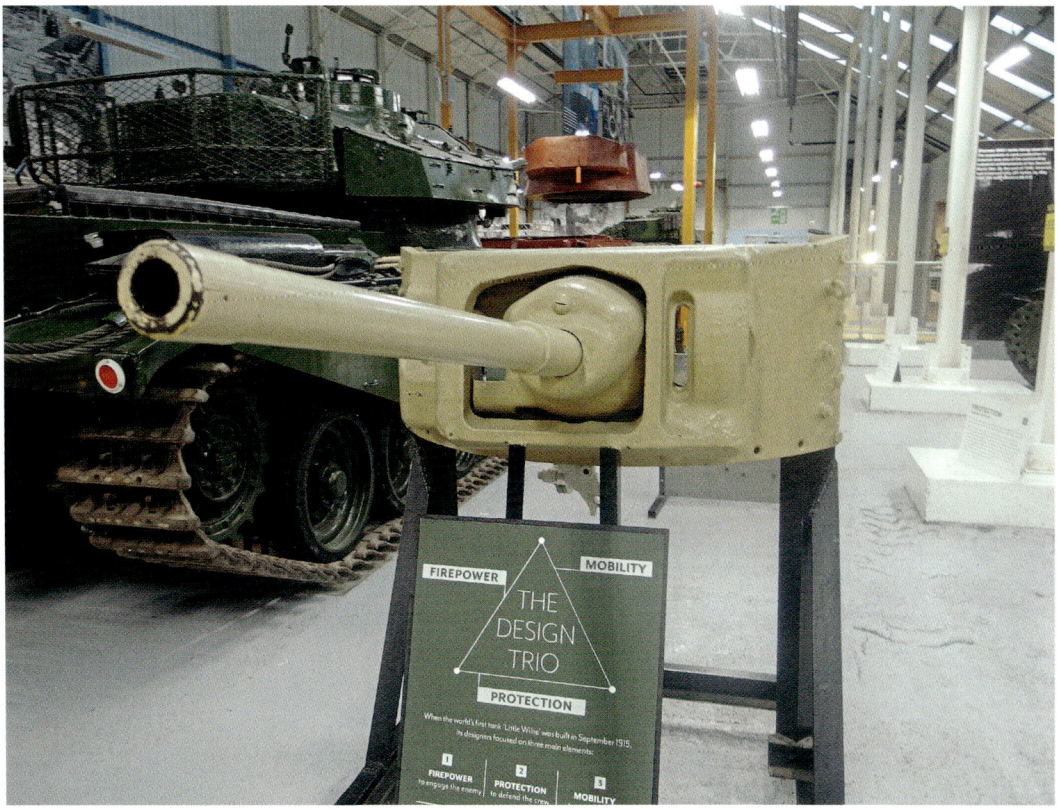

Gun mount used on Valentine III and Valentine V tanks, Bovington Tank Museum. The gun was moved much further forward than on the Valentine I or II in order to make space for the tank commander.

even TM6117 was altered before it was completed. A total of 699 Valentine III tanks were built.

Just as the Valentine II was supplanted by the Valentine IV with an American engine, so the Valentine III was supplanted by the Valentine V. The first contract for 755 Valentine V tanks with GM 6004 engines was signed with Vickers on May 7, 1941. Four hundred tanks were built under contract T2455, although it initially stipulated 755 tanks. Contract T2454 originally calling for Valentine II from Metropolitan Cammell Carriage & Wagon Company was responsible for the majority of Valentine V tanks. 545 Valentine Vs were built here, plus 25 three-man turrets without tanks for training. Contract TM6118 was for 455 tanks, but only 127 of these ended up being Valentine Vs.

The first Valentine tanks with three-man turrets arrived in the USSR with convoy PQ-16 in June 1942. These were all Valentine Vs. More Valentine V tanks were loaded onto the infamous convoy PQ-17, which took heavy losses in transit. Deliveries of British tanks slowed down to a trickle. A small number of tanks arrived with convoy JW-51B in January. This shipment also included Valentine III tanks. A mix of Valentine tanks, including the III and V, arrived through the Arctic route in February 1943. A long pause followed. JW-54

Valentine V tank, Museum of National Military History. Valentines III and V featured an enlarged turret that could fit a third crewman, although it was a tight fit. PAVEL BOROVIKOV

brought 37 Valentine III and 42 Valentine V tanks in December 1943, after which delivery slowed down. Only 61 Valentine IIIs and 50 Valentine Vs arrived via Arctic convoys in 1944.[45]

Valentine tanks also arrived through Iran. These tanks were heavily used, as they were missing parts and had obvious damage. They began to arrive in July 1943 in small batches. Fifty-one Valentine IIIs and 16 Valentine Vs were delivered. In addition to tanks shipped specifically for the USSR, the British shared vehicles that were already on location. In April 1944, the British informed the Red Army that 90 tanks including Valentine Vs formerly used in Iraq could be handed over. The condition of these tanks was extremely poor and they had to be refurbished in Baku before being forwarded up north. The last 11 tanks, all used, were delivered on September 30, 1944. This was the last shipment of Valentine tanks to arrive in the USSR.[46] 340 Valentine V tanks were sent to the USSR, of which 113 were lost en route. The Valentine III was more common, with 346 tanks shipped and no losses in transit.[47]

Canadian Valentines: VI, VII, and VIIA

Unlike Great Britain, Canada entered the Second World War without a tank building tradition. Tank forces raised in the First World War never saw battle and the country had nearly no armoured vehicles by the end of the 1930s. The Department of National

Valentine tank, Base Borden. Canadian Valentine tanks with a BESA machine gun were designated Valentine VI, while tanks with a Browning machine gun were designated Valentine VII.

Defence purchased 14 Vickers Light Tank Mk.VIB in 1938-39, but these lightly armoured vehicles armed only with machine guns were already looking pretty weak compared to the tanks seen in Europe.

The Canadian government began to seriously consider composing an armoured force after the fall of Poland. Mechanisation of the cavalry units of both the Permanent Militia and the Non-Permanent Active Militia was proposed. 219 Light Tanks M1917 were purchased from the United States at scrap value, but these were nearly useless and could at best be used to train, not to fight. Canada needed to set up its own tank production if it wanted to equip its tankers.[48]

There was a great deal to choose from, although it didn't take long for potential candidates to appear. The British proposed that Canada could build 100-200 Infantry Tanks Mk.III for their army, after which production could continue to equip Canadian forces.[49] This was far from the only option. Technical specifications of the Infantry Tanks Mk.I through Mk.IV[50] and Cruiser Tanks Mk.IV through Mk.VI were sent to Canada. The French SOMUA S 35 and Char B1 as well as the American Medium Tank M2 were also considered.[51]

The Infantry Tank Mk.I was discarded almost immediately as unsatisfactory. The Mk.II was better, but it was heavy, complex, and had high ground pressure. The

Valentine VIIA, Canadian War Museum. The most obvious change was the introduction of a cast front hull instead of a bolted one, but many other improvements were introduced compared to early Valentines.

Infantry Tanks Mk.III and Mk.IV were the favourites of this race. A faction in the Canadian military including Brigadier Pratt and General McNoughton favoured the latter, preferring the latest and greatest in tank technology. However, this was not the best choice. The design of the Infantry Tank Mk.IV was not finished and it would take months before any blueprints could be sent to Canada. Time was of the essence, since it would take several years to spin up tank production in a country with limited heavy industry. The 16-ton Infantry Tank Mk.III was the only possible option.

The British War Ministry expanded its contract for Valentine tanks in Canada to 300 units on June 7, 1940.[52] Preparations for production were already underway. The British allocated a sum of three million Canadian dollars to equip Canadian factories, but in the meantime it was acceptable to order parts from the United States. Captain F. W. Jones, a Canadian officer, was sent to the UK to study its tank industry, inspecting the Vickers-Armstrongs factory and proving grounds at Farnborough.[53]

This American influence left a mark on the Canadian Valentine. Not only did it use a GM 6004 engine, but also a coaxial Browning machine gun instead of a British BESA (although early tanks built in Canada still had BESAs).[54] A Valentine tank with

The same tank as seen from above. The turret was a tight fit, offering just enough room for two men and their weapons.

registration number T.16356 was sent to Canada to serve as a reference. It also had an American diesel engine.[55]

The Angus Shops of the Canadian Pacific Rail (CPR) company were chosen to build the Valentine tank. The company promised to begin delivering tanks in March of 1941 and complete their order for 300 tanks by September. Plans only grew from there. Canada considered ordering an additional 488 tanks to equip its own military,[56] but the British stepped in and claimed all tanks coming out of CPR with the exception of 30 Valentines that Canada was allowed to keep.[57]

As it often happens, these prognoses were very optimistic. The first Valentine tank was shown to the press in a grandiose ceremony in the spring of 1941 but then quietly withdrawn by the factory, as assembly was still incomplete. True mass production began by the fall, but still fell short of projections. Angus Shops delivered 14 tanks in September out of the expected 47. These delays were a major reason why the Canadians never went into battle in their own tanks.[58]

When the Infantry Tank Mk.III officially became the Valentine on September 23, 1941, tanks built in Canada received a separate index. Tanks with GMC engines and BESA machine guns were designated Valentine VI and tanks with Browning machine guns

Close up of the Valentine's 40mm 2-pounder gun. Canada only built tanks with 2-pounders, even though the 6-pounder became available before production ended.

became Valentine VII. Valentine VI tanks had WD numbers in the T.23204-T.23218 range and the Valentine VII fell between T.21219-T-23503 and T.73554-T.74193.[59] Later tanks with improvements similar to the Valentine IV and cast front hulls were named Valentine VIIA. British documents do not differentiate between these types of tanks, usually grouping them together under the term 'Canadian Valentine'.[60]

Despite the interest shown in Canadian Valentines by the British, they did not have the opportunity to use them either. Deliveries of Canadian tanks began when the USSR's need for tanks was the greatest, and so Canadian Valentines went to fight for the Red Army. The first 15 tanks were delivered before a unified inventory system was created in November 1941. Thirty more tanks were allocated in November, 55 in December, 78 in January and February of 1942, 80 in March and April, 90 in May and June, 110 in August and 120 in September. These optimistic projections were not met.[61] The allocation requirement was later lowered to 75 tanks per month.[62]

In total, Canada built 956 Valentine tanks in 1941-42 and 464 in 1943. Production of the Valentine in Canada ended in June 1943, but deliveries lagged behind production. The last 10 Canadian Valentines were sent to the USSR in November 1943 and arrived in Baku by March.[63] A total of 1,388 Valentine tanks were shipped from Canada to the USSR and 1,041 arrived at their destination.[64]

The first 15 Valentine VI tanks were sent to the USSR in November 1941 on SS *City of Flint* and arrived in Murmansk on

Drop tank, shown here on a Valentine IX tank. This tank contained enough diesel to drive an extra 80km before refuelling, but also impeded turret traverse. PIERRE-OLIVIER BUAN

February 22, 1942, as a part of convoy PQ-11. Fifty-five Valentine VII tanks came with convoy PQ-13 soon after. Soviet QA noticed that Canadian tanks were packed with winter conditions in mind and their cooling systems survived the journey without problems. However, aluminium parts were used in the running gear which corroded when exposed to seawater. Seventy Valentines arrived with PQ-15 and 40 more with PQ-16, including Valentine VIIA tanks. Soviet records made a note of the different variants.[65]

After the destruction of convoy PQ-17, deliveries of Valentine VII tanks continued only through Iran. The first six Canadian tanks arrived in Baku by September 1, 1942.

323 Canadian Valentine tanks arrived in the USSR in 1942 and 709 in 1943.[66]

The changes to Canadian Valentine tanks were covered in detail by the head of the Soviet acceptance commission at the Angus Shops, Captain Sokolov, in a report composed on November 7, 1942. Sokolov wrote that the most noticeable change was the 26 gallon drop tank on the left side of the hull. The extra fuel lasted for 80km of driving, making the overall cruising range 230km. The driver could jettison the tank by pulling a lever. The tank was hooked up to the fuel system and fuel from there was used up first. This tank could be knocked off by turning the gun backwards, so Sokolov warned crews to either drop the tank before entering combat or not lower the gun past horizontal in the third quadrant of rotation.[67]

There was another visual difference. Most tanks from the series (##821-839 and ##895-1420) had angle irons welded to the turret platform to protect the turret ring. The turret ring was also reinforced.

There were plenty of less visible changes introduced during production. Tanks after T.23335 had four 6V batteries instead of two 12V. The electrical system was rearranged to load the batteries more evenly. New tanks also had a convoy light, although the first tanks of the series lacked it due to shortages. The Valentine VIIA had the same Wireless Set No.19 as the Valentine VII, but unlike its predecessor it was no longer possible to install the older Wireless Set No.11 as of tank T.23334. In case a replacement was required, Sokolov suggested swapping radios with an earlier tank and installing its Wireless Set No.19 into a new one.

The Valentine VIIA also had smoke grenade launchers installed over the transmission compartment fired via buttons on the driver's console. Other changes included a new mechanical emergency engine shutoff instead of the old electromagnetic one, a new arrangement of the water-cooling system, an oil radiator, and a new instrument panel for the driver, which included a compass. The hand fuel pump for starting the tank in cold weather was removed from the console and moved behind the driver. The driver's seat was simplified and his controls were improved. There were also improvements made to the suspension, running gear, turret traverse motor, and firing mechanisms. A change in ammunition racks increased the amount of ammo carried for the Bren gun from 700 to 764 rounds.[68]

Since Soviet QA differentiated between Canadian Valentines and British ones, separate trials were held for the Valentine VII. Tank T.23383 was selected. This example was built in January 1942 and had arrived in the USSR with convoy PQ-15 on May 5.

The tank's engine was tuned to deliver 165hp instead of the stock 130hp stated in the manual. The tank drove for 1,360km of trials like this, giving an average speed of 18.8kph, burning 163L of diesel per 100km of driving for a cruising range of 105km. The power was then lowered to 130hp, which reduced the average speed to 17.3kph but also improved fuel economy to 153L per 100km and increased the cruising range to 115km. Testers noted that the economy was small, but the mobility of the tank decreased noticeably. The average speed on a highway was 25kph and testers managed to accelerate the tank up to 26.4kph. The Valentine only drove for 160km on a stone road with the rest of the trials conducted on dirt roads and cross-country.[69]

The Valentine VII also took part in comparative trials with German and American tanks. It turned out that even though the Valentine had the lowest top speed, its average speed on a highway was the same as for the Pz.Kpfw.38(t) Ausf.F. Off-road mobility was superior to the Pz.Kpfw.38(t) and Medium Tank M3, at the cost of burning slightly more fuel. The Canadian tank was also quite competitive when it came to driving uphill with a maximum slope of 32°. The engine could have handled a steeper slope, but the tracks slipped. The tracks also limited the tank's ability to drive at a tilt, slipping off after an angle of 26°.[70]

The performance of the Valentine VII during river crossings was also good. Even though it was the lowest of all the competitors, it could confidently cross a 1,400mm deep river, only stalling when reversing. Neither the Pz.Kpfw.38(t) nor

The Valentine's suspension offered good off-road mobility and the tracks were wide enough to carry the 16-ton tank through mud and swamps.

the Pz.Kpfw.III Ausf.H used in the trials managed to make the crossing at all.[71] The Valentine VII also had the lowest ground pressure among its competitors at 0.6kg/cm², which allowed it to cross a section of swamp in second gear without difficulty. The tank only bottomed out when driving in a depression left by another tank, but even then it could free itself with the use of an unditching log. The Light Tank M3 and Pz.Kpfw.38(t) could also cross this swamp, but the Medium Tank M3 and Pz.Kpfw.III could not, even with the aid of a log.[72]

Conclusions to the trial praised the tank: "Despite its low power to weight ratio and maximum speed, the tank has a relatively high average speed, thanks to a fortunate construction of its gearbox and high quality of the GMC diesel engine."[73]

Winter trials were held separately, from January to March 1943. The same Valentine VII tank took part in comparative trials with a Valentine II. These trials were 1,161km long for a total distance of 3,019km. The GM engine turned out to be more reliable than the AEC A190. The Valentine VII was also faster, but burned more fuel.[74]

Coincidentally, the Canadians also decided to test their tank in winter conditions at the same time. These trials were conducted at Camp Shilo in Manitoba, a popular site for cold weather training. Standard diesel fuel with a flame primer worked at temperatures over -20°F (-29°C). If the tank was filled with kerosene, it would start even at -25°F (-32°C). Ethyl ether had to be used to start the engine at lower temperatures. With proper lubrication, the transmission operated at temperatures as low as -43°F (-42°C).

The turret ring would seize up at

temperatures below -10°F (-23°C) unless the grease was thinned with kerosene. A mix of lubricants also allowed the gun to work at temperatures over -30°F (-34°C). The report also noted that batteries should be held outside of the tank in a warm place and charged as often as possible. Performance of the running gear was satisfactory. Spurs could hold the tank at a slope of up to 11°, but did not help against sliding perpendicular to the direction of movement. The spurs also decreased the tank's speed, but not by a lot.[75]

Firepower Upgrade: Valentine IX and X

While the 2-pounder was a powerful weapon for its time, it would not remain competitive forever. Trials against the latest German tanks in North Africa held in the summer of 1941 showed that 2-pounder shot could penetrate the front of a Pz.Kpfw.IV tank with applique armour (30 + 30mm) from 500 yards away[76] and the front of a Pz.Kpfw.III tank (50mm) from just 100 yards.[77]

The appearance of such tanks was not a surprise for the British. The A12E1 prototype that entered trials back in 1938 was already highly resistant to the 2-pounder gun. It was only a matter of time before the enemy would field a tank with comparable protection. Work on a gun to combat these prospective tanks began in 1938 and received approval by the General Staff in December of 1939. The gun was designated Ordnance QF 6-pdr 7 cwt. Unlike the short-barrelled 6-pounder of the First World War, this was a high velocity weapon capable of penetrating 70mm of armour sloped at 20° at a range of 1,100 yards (1,000m). While development of this gun was rather sluggish, it was the weapon of choice for both the next generation of British tanks and modernisations of existing vehicles, including the Valentine.[78]

The 6-pounder gun was considerably larger than the 2-pounder, which meant that a new turret was required to house it. The three-man turret of the Valentine III was taken as a starting point. The third crewman, 2in bomb thrower, and even the coaxial machine gun were removed to make room for the gun. The ability to fire smoke bombs was preserved with externally mounted launchers, but the only weapon remaining that could fight infantry was the Bren gun on the Lakeman Mounting. Since this was primarily an anti-aircraft weapon, the angle of depression did not exceed 2-3° past horizontal.

The location of the mounting also limited the traverse of the weapon without moving the whole turret.[79] The commander's cupola disappeared along with the commander. Instead, there were now two hatches on the roof. Visibility was maintained with three rotating periscopes. Two periscopes pointed forward and one to the rear right, giving the commander (who doubled as the loader) good visibility backwards.[80]

The tank with a 6-pounder gun and AEC A190 engine was named Valentine VIII and the variant with the American GM 6004 diesel engine was named Valentine IX. Since production of the Valentine tank switched to using American engines exclusively, the Valentine VIII was never built. To compensate for the tank's increased weight, the GM 6004 on the Valentine IX was equipped with a more powerful injector for an output of 165hp at 1,900rpm.[81]

Contracts for the Valentine IX were signed in the fall of 1941 with MCCW and Elswick Works. Production began a year later without a prototype, but a sample was still sent to the artillery proving grounds at Lulworth for testing. The tank gave a good showing, proving capable of hitting stationary and moving targets at a range of 1,500 yards when firing from a standstill or 700 yards on the move.[82] The new gun vented more fumes into the turret when

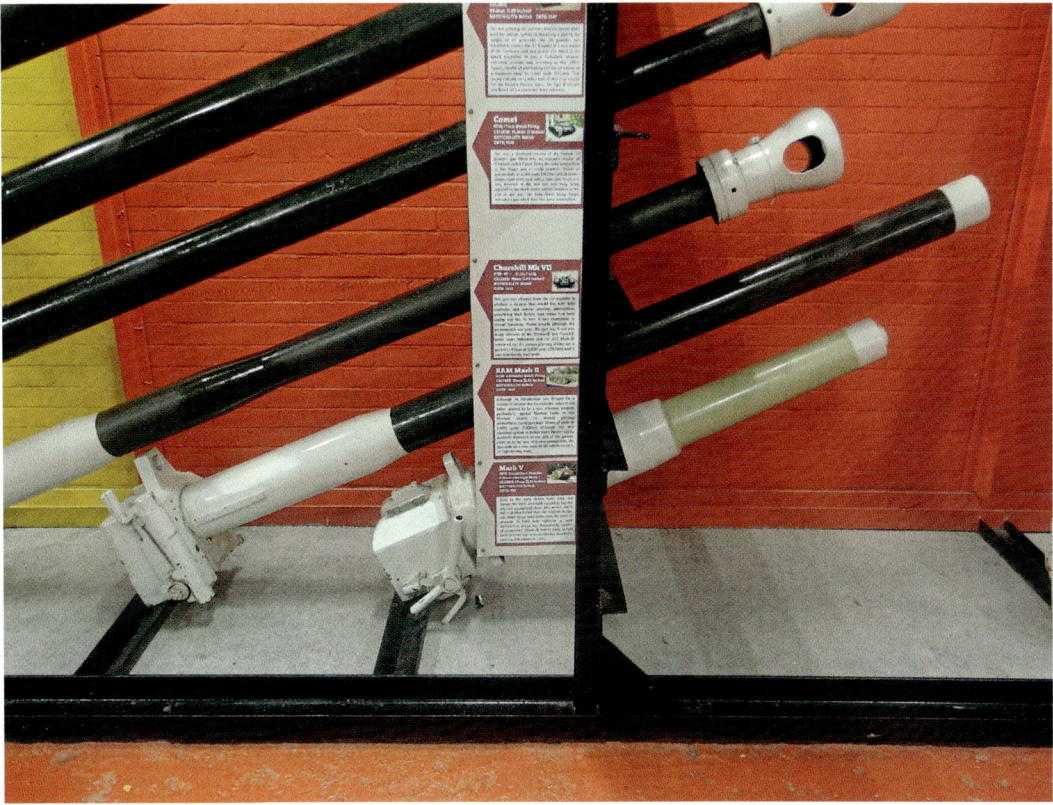

Display of tank guns at the Bovington Tank Museum showing the difference between a short 6-pounder gun used on WWI era tanks (bottom) and the longer 6-pounder Mk.III used on several WWII era tanks (second from the bottom). The Valentine IX and X used the 6-pounder Mk.V with an even longer barrel.

it fired than the 2-pounder. Due to a poor design and unfortunate position the single ventilation fan did not circulate enough air to keep the concentration of CO in the turret below dangerous levels. The fan circulated only 20 cfm per minute, while 150 cfm were needed to keep the air breathable. At this rate, the crew would suffer the effects of CO poisoning after firing one shot per minute for one hour. If the engine was running at maximum RPM with the intake louvres open, it could suck out enough fumes out of the fighting compartment to keep the crew safe. Trials also showed that the new gun mantlet left much to be desired, as it let splash through and could be jammed by armour piercing or even regular bullets. Nevertheless, the upgraded gun kept the Valentine tank competitive on the battlefield.[83]

The USSR learned about the new type of tank in December 1942 and the reaction was mixed. On one hand, a new more powerful gun was welcomed. The 6-pounder Mk.V gun penetrated up to 101mm of armour sloped at 30° at point-blank range, which made it a useful weapon against any known German tank.[84] On the other hand, the new tank weighed an estimated 18-19 tons, which threatened to decrease the vehicle's service life. The fact that the Valentine IX went into

Valentine IX tank, Bovington Tank Museum. This variant received the powerful 57mm 6-pounder Mk.V gun, but lost its coaxial machine gun and 2in bomb thrower. PIERRE-OLIVIER BUAN

production immediately without a prototype was even more reason for caution.[85]

The first Valentine IX tanks arrived with convoy JW-52 in January 1943. Only a handful of tanks with 6-pounder guns were ordered for evaluation and most Valentines that came with this convoy were older models. A Valentine IX with WD number T.122725 was sent to the NIBT proving grounds for testing on March 14 and first impressions were positive. The new Valentine weighed not 19 tons as expected, but just 17. This was the same as a Valentine III and a bit heavier than a Valentine II. The savings in weight were achieved in part by the thinning out of the side armour from 60 to 50mm.

Mobility trials also assuaged the Soviets' fears. The Valentine IX made a 500km drive to the NIBT Proving Grounds under its own power, demonstrating an average movement speed of 20.9kph on a highway, slightly better than the Valentine II achieved in trials. Off-road, the average speed was comparable (12-16kph for the Valentine IX and 12-15 for the Valentine II). There were some minor breakdowns experienced during the march, but none of them were caused by the extra stress on the suspension. The tank burned 131L of fuel per 100km of driving on a clear highway and 136L if the highway was covered in snow. This gave a cruising range of up to 240km.[86]

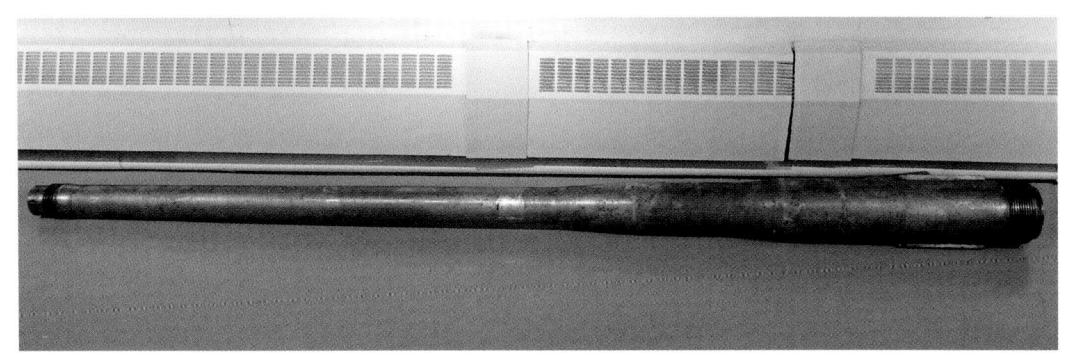

6-pounder Mk.V gun barrel, Base Borden. The threaded muzzle allowed for the installation of a counterweight or muzzle brake, making it easy to install and balance the 6-pounder gun on a number of different armoured vehicles.

Gunnery trials were carried out separately. The tank fired at 4x6m targets from a range of 500 and 1,000 yards (457 and 914m) both while standing and on the move. In these trials, the gunner fired 10 shots with no limit on the time taken to aim. The precision of the gun was very high with a probable error of 11cm vertically and 8cm horizontally at 500 yards and 18cm vertically and 16 horizontally at 1,000 yards. This meant that the gunner would have no difficulty hitting a tank-sized target. Like the British, the Soviets tested the tank's ability to fire on the move. At a speed of 10kph, the tank achieved a probable error of 95cm vertically and 75cm horizontally against targets 400-500 yards away. The Soviets blamed this result on the stiff suspension and poor traction of the tracks, as the vehicle swayed considerably when driving. Nevertheless, the gunner would have a fair chance of hitting an enemy tank at this range.

A separate trial was held to establish the maximum aimed rate of fire in five-round bursts. Standing still, the crew fired five shots at a target located 1,000 yards away and hit three times for a ROF of 10rpm and 60% hit rate. At a speed of 9-10kph, the rate of fire dropped to an average of 2.7rpm and hit rate to 20%. The crew could fire twice per minute when moving at 15kph, but did not score any hits.[87]

A second Valentine IX was tested at the NIBT Proving Grounds in August 1943. This tank had additional cleats on each track link, since the Red Army was complaining about insufficient traction on British vehicles. Trials showed that this feature did not help very much. The speed and fuel consumption for tanks with cleats and without were about the same. The tank's performance on a slope increased slightly: a Valentine IX without cleats began to slip at a climb of 30°, and one with cleats slipped only at 32°. A tank without cleats could drive at a tilt of 29°, while one with cleats held on at up to 30° before slipping.

The lifespan of the cleats was very short. After driving for 251km on a paved road, the cleats were worn down by 8-10mm. Reports from the front lines also indicated that the cleats tore up roads, making them useless after tanks had passed by. The cleats also destroyed railway platforms when used to transport the tanks. The testers theorised that the cleats could come in handy when driving on ice and instructed crews to only leave them on every fifth track to preserve roads and transport equipment.[88]

The British were just as upset as the Soviets that the Valentine lost its coaxial machine gun and worked on a solution. It turned out to be possible to install a BESA machine gun into a bulge into the front of the turret. The gun was not strictly speaking coaxial, as it could be unlinked from the main gun and aimed independently. The new tank was indexed Valentine X and went through testing at Lulworth in early June 1943. The machine gun turned out to be unbalanced and the default position of the box with the ammunition belt got in the way of both the loader and the gunner. Nevertheless, the new variant of the tank was positively received.[89]

Valentine X tanks were shipped to the USSR starting in January 1944. A Valentine X with WD number T.123484 arrived as a part of convoy JW-56A and was forwarded to the NIBT Proving Grounds for trials. The GBTU showed little interest in this tank and did not carry out complete trials. Only a brief inspection was performed. Soviet specialists noted that due to the presence of a machine gun and 1,800 rounds of ammunition for it, the amount of ammunition for the main gun was reduced to 44 rounds. The Valentine X was quite rare with only 135 built. No new contracts were signed for it; instead, existing contracts for the Valentine IX were altered to produce it. Seventy-four tanks were sent to the USSR and 66 reached their destination.[90] Only a handful of photos of this tank in Soviet service are known today. The Valentine IX was much more common as 836 were sent to the USSR out of a total of 1,011.[91]

Soviet Upgrades

As mentioned previously, the Red Army was dissatisfied with the 2-pounder gun. No HE shell was available for it, and even AP shot was supplied in only limited quantities. There was also a shortage of spare barrels. It was therefore suggested that the Valentine could be armed with a Soviet gun, the same as with the Matilda. The Valentine's turret was smaller than the Matilda's, so a 45mm gun was chosen as a replacement. Factory #92 was tasked with building a prototype in November 1941. A Valentine II with WD number T.27526 was allocated for the conversion. The 45mm gun adapted for the Valentine was indexed F-95. Just like the Matilda's F-96, the coaxial BESA was replaced with a DT machine gun.

The new tank was an improvement over the original. The gun mantlet developed at factory #92 was better protected against splash. The 45mm gun and its brass catcher were more compact than the 2-pounder, which freed up space in the turret. A better laid-out ammo rack allowed the tank to carry 91 45mm rounds compared to 59 shots for the 2-pounder. Trials showed that the new ammo racks did not get in the way of either the gunner or the loader.

A 20km trial run did not reveal any defects in the mountings of the gun or the sight. The tank was even shown to the Soviet government and approved for production, but GABTU Chief Lieutenant General Fedorenko stepped in. His reasons for opposing the project were largely the same as for the Matilda. The stated goal of freeing the tankers from dependence on British-made ammo was no longer all that important, as supplies of ammunition greatly improved. The firepower of the tank did not meaningfully increase with the installation of a 45mm gun, as the penetration of the Soviet 20-K and British 2-pounder was roughly the same. The lack of an HE shell was a valid complaint, but just as with the Matilda there was simply no manpower or spare 45mm guns available to complete the conversion.[92]

Nevertheless, while the Matilda did get its HE thanks to Close Support tanks, tankers in Valentines felt left out. There were efforts to correct this drawback however, and one solution was quite ingenious. British tanks commonly came equipped with 2in bomb throwers designed to fire smoke bombs. At a calibre of 51.25mm, the launcher was just large enough to accept ammunition from the Soviet 50mm company mortar. Trials were carried out by the 593rd Independent Tank Battalion of the Transcaucasian Front on September 8, 1942. The British launchers fired the Soviet 850g shell to a range of 300-500m. The trial was deemed a success and the Armoured Vehicle Directorate of the Transcaucasian Front issued a request to the artillery branch for 60 mortar shells per tank to be issued to three tank battalions.[93]

Another attempt to equip the Valentine with HE was undertaken at a higher level two months later. The Deputy Chief of the Red Army GAU (Main Artillery Directorate) Lieutenant General of Artillery Hohlov approved trials which involved converting ammunition from a British 40mm AA gun to be fired from the 2-pounder gun. These were going to be much more detailed than simply sticking the shell in and seeing how far it flew. Hohlov ordered crimped and uncrimped rounds to be carefully monitored during repeated loading and unloading, measurements of the rifling and driving band to ensure compatibility, and calculations to determine the maximum permissible pressure when using this kind of ammunition. The goal was to create a high explosive shell with a muzzle velocity of 790m/s operating at a safe pressure, whether by using British propellant taken from the shells disassembled from conversion or equivalent Soviet propellant.[94] The author does not possess information on the results of these trials, but if this solution was put into use, it was not widespread.

This was not the last time someone attempted to toy with the Valentine's armament in Soviet service. Since the delivery of Valentine tanks armed with 2-pounder guns continued well past the obsolescence of the weapon, it seemed reasonable to perform a modernisation, especially considering that the British themselves had upgraded their tanks with the more powerful 6-pounder. This idea was put forward by Major General Alymov, the head of the GBTU's Self Propelled Artillery directorate. Alymov wrote a proposal to the same factory #92 that rearmed the Matilda and Valentine some two years prior. Alymov aimed high, as the weapon he picked for installation was not a 45mm or even a 76mm gun. Rather, Major General Alymov proposed installing the 85mm S-53 into the turret of the Valentine and with a coaxial DT machine gun to boot.

Alymov's requirement for 360° turret traverse confirms that his idea was not a fixed casemate tank destroyer like the Archer either, but a proper turreted tank.[95] While the S-53 was quite a compact weapon and could even fit into the two-man turret of the T-34 tank, there were some difficulties with handling the longer 85mm round in such a confined space.[96] The T-34 tank with a 76mm gun had a turret ring clearance of 1,420mm. The Valentine's turret ring was just 1,270mm wide.[97] It is not clear how Alymov expected a loader to handle a 95cm long round[98] in such close quarters and it does not appear that this proposal gained any traction.

The gun was not the only element of the tank to get attention from Soviet tankers looking to improve their vehicles. As mentioned above, the Valentine was not designed for fighting in harsh winters and performed poorly in snow and ice. Reports on tanks slipping and sliding on icy roads were filed even before trials at the NIBT Proving Grounds confirmed that the tank lacked traction in winter conditions. In good conditions, it could climb a 25° slope, but in

Valentine II tank, Patriot Park. This tank has several 30mm thick armour plates welded to it to improve its protection. PAVEL BOROVIKOV

winter this limit was cut by more than half. Since the Valentine clearly had the engine power required to pull itself up hills, the problem was with the tracks.

Two potential solutions came from a participant in testing of foreign tanks at the NIBT Proving Grounds, Military Engineer 2nd Class Anatoliy Mikhailovich Zezin. One was quite simple: two spurs 35mm deep were welded onto a track link. This was a secure method of attachment, but also quite permanent. The only way to remove the spurs would be to replace the link. The other method was more advanced. The spur was attached to the track pin and set in between the track links. This was the preferable method, since the spur was removable, had a better design, and there was no need to modify the track links.

A trials report signed on April 29, 1942, describes both designs as quite effective and long lasting. Unfortunately, the coming summer deprioritised any attempt to improve performance in winter and it appears that Zezin's spurs were forgotten by the winter of 1942-43. The item was not mentioned in the summary report on work completed at the NIBT Proving Grounds in 1942.[99]

Even though Zezin's spurs were not put into production, they were not forgotten entirely. Engineer-Captain I. A. Kondrashev and Technician-Lieutenant

A. S. Lobakov picked up where Zezin left off. A variant of Zezin's spur with a toothed grouser was tested. With eight spurs per side, Kondrashev's design increased the maximum slope a Valentine could climb to 24-25°, almost as high as on good terrain. Unfortunately, the trials documentation was only completed in May 1943 and the idea was forgotten until the late fall when a third idea was submitted by inventor Zakharnikov, who proposed welding a waved strip of metal to the tracks. The GBTU rejected this suggestion and suddenly remembered that they had a better one in store.[100]

An order was given in December 1943 to produce a trial batch. There is no information about how widespread this solution was, but Zezin, Kondrashev, and Lobakov received a bonus of 1,000 rubles each on March 9, 1944. It would seem that the solution was found to be useful.[101] That being said, the four men mentioned in this book were far from the only ones to have thought of the idea of improving mobility of foreign tanks. Various techniques including welding fragments of broken track pins to the bottom of track links were practised with Sherman tanks;[102] Marshal of the Soviet Union I. A. Yakubovsky recalls in his memoirs that he ordered cleats to be riveted to the tracks of his Churchill tanks.[103]

The armour of the Valentine tank was another aspect that could be improved. While higher ranking officials were concerned about keeping the weight of the tank low to avoid overloading the chassis, frontline tankers and commanders were more concerned with survival. One of these commanders was Engineer-Major A. G. Aranovich, Technical Deputy Commander of the 167th Tank Brigade. Aranovich was closely involved with the repair of knocked out Valentines and took notice of the weakest parts of the armour. The turret of the tanks often jammed due to a lack of splash protection for the turret rings.

Thanks to the increasing number of 75mm Pak 40 anti-tank guns on the battlefield, the front of the tank was penetrated more and more often. In November 1942, Aranovich wrote to the GABTU with a proposal for an up-armouring scheme. A collar made up of sections of armour was bolted to the perimeter of the turret, protecting the turret ring. Fragments of rubber tyres were placed between the main armour and the collar to absorb the shock from a hit. If the collar armour was damaged, the section could easily be replaced.

Aranovich also protected the front of the tank. 45mm applique armour was added at a slope of 30° to the front of the hull and turret platform. This gave the tank protection comparable to that of the heavy KV-1S tank. According to Aranovich's report, this solution was tested in combat when his brigade was fighting at Stalingrad. Unfortunately for Aranovich, the GABTU showed little interest. His idea was waved off to the Department of Inventions, the branch of the GABTU chiefly responsible for handling well-meaning individuals pitching death rays and perpetual motion machines.[104]

The fact that this refusal was an error can be seen in the prevalence of unofficial armour improvement schemes. These modifications were never officially reported, which is why we do not know their inventors nor the precise dates when they were implemented. However, photographs and at least one surviving tank serve as records of these modifications. A Valentine tank with WD number T.27543 currently on display at Patriot Park has enhanced frontal armour and a collar around the turret ring. However, this modification was much simpler than what Aranovich proposed. Sections of metal were welded to the turret platform to protect the turret ring from jamming, but only partially.

30mm thick plates were welded to the front of the turret platform and hull front. Dents in the applique armour show that it came in handy at least once. Unfortunately, there is no way to tell for sure when or where the tank fought.

A photo exists showing a number of tanks with similar modifications, but its precise date and location are also unknown. Photos of tanks with simpler modifications also pop up. A Valentine IV with applique armour on the hull but no collar was photographed in Vilnius in 1944, as well as a Valentine IX and X near Magdeburg in 1945.[105] One can confidently say that despite a lack of official approval, many Soviet tank commanders identified both the need for additional armour and took advantage of the ability of the Valentine tank chassis to carry extra 30-45mm plates on the front.[106]

As with many other tanks, chassis in good condition with irreparable damage to the turret or simply tanks that were otherwise obsolete were converted into prime movers. This practice started in August 1944 at the latest, when repair factory #12 in Baku reported a "MK-III prime mover" in its inventory. Repair factory #82 in Moscow leaned into this practice, converting two tanks in April 1945, 11 in June, and 14 in July.[107]

Fifty-four functional Valentine tanks were reported to still be in the possession of the Soviet Armoured and Mechanised Forces as of November 17, 1947. Marshal of the Armoured Forces S. Bogdanov reported that there was a standing order to prohibit the transfer of tanks to the agricultural sector and instead use them in the army to make up for a shortage of prime movers. Despite his protests, 10 tanks were authorised to be transferred to the Ministry of Machine and Instrument Building and 50 tanks to the Ministry of Transport Machine Building.[108] While not as popular as prime movers on the Medium Tank M4A2 chassis, Valentines continued to serve the Soviet Union even after the conclusion of the Second World War.

Infantry Tank Mk.IV (Churchill)

Churchill I-IV

The tank that came to be known as the Churchill emerged from a programme to create a heavy tank not dissimilar to the ones used in the First World War. The concept began to form in September 1939, when the next World War was already starting, but there was no indication yet as to what kind of war it was going to be. In case the new war was anything like the last one, the General Staff asked for a tank with thick armour that would withstand the German 37mm anti-tank gun. The tank had to operate on even the roughest terrain pock-marked with shell craters with the use of an unditching beam, meaning that much like the tanks of the First World War its tracks had to wrap all the way around the hull. Much like those tanks, the main guns would be housed in sponsons. This tank was indexed A20.[109]

Thankfully, the A20E1 prototype built by the Harland & Wolff shipyard was considerably more modern. No sponsons were installed, and the tank instead sported a turret borrowed from the Infantry Tank Mk.II. The prototype failed trials in part due to gearbox trouble, but the concept of a 40 ton heavily armoured tank was

Infantry Tank Mk.IV or Churchill I, Base Borden. This is one of the two Churchill tanks sent to Canada for trials. The Churchill was a very temperamental machine, and thus winter trials were necessary to make sure that tanks sent to the Soviet Union worked as expected.

generally considered workable.[110] A new set of requirements was developed under the index A22. The project was passed on from Harland & Wolff to Vauxhall Motors in July 1940. This was a risky move, as the firm had initially only proposed a new engine for the A20 and had never built tanks at all.[111]

The requirements for the new tank were quite loose. The most important thing was that 500 tanks could be produced within the next 12 months. The General Staff feared a German invasion and were happy to get a heavily armoured tank no matter what. Their level of desperation could be felt in the requirement that "they would be acceptable even if they could run only 50 miles or even only 10 miles".[112]

The General Staff didn't get their 500 tanks, but a prototype of the tank was ready by December 1940[113] and 14 tanks were delivered by June 1941.[114] Despite the tank's classification as a production model, the design of the vehicle now designated Infantry Tank Mk.IV remained in flux, as Vauxhall was desperately trying to iron out the numerous teething troubles of their new machine.[115]

The tank was a mix of new and old solutions. The tracks wrapped around the entire hull, but the main gun was carried in a turret alongside three crewmen. No sponsons were fitted, although the tank had large doors with pistol ports in its sides. A 3in howitzer was placed in the hull, fired and loaded by the assistant driver. The tank could also carry a second BESA machine gun in the hull instead of a howitzer. This variant was dubbed Infantry Tank Mk.IVA.[116] The turret only carried a 2-pounder gun, as no larger weapon was available. The 38-ton tank was armed about as well as the much lighter infantry tanks already in service.

The armour of the Infantry Tank Mk.IV was much more impressive. The cast turret walls were 95mm thick.[117] The hull was a more complex arrangement, consisting of 63.5mm thick armoured steel plate held on to a 12.7mm thick carbon-manganese steel 'skin' with 2in thick screws. The 'skin' was in turn backed with a frame made from mild steel. This kind of multi-layer system was necessary to prevent the hull from falling apart under fire, as otherwise even relatively minor deformations of the inner plate would tear out the screws. As it stood, the tank was considered immune to hits from 2-pounder shot at ranges of over 400 yards.[118]

The biggest problem with this tank was its poor reliability. The lifespan of the Bedford Twin Six engine was measured at a mere nine hours.[119] The tracks and running gear were good for 20-50 miles of driving.[120] Vauxhall included a notice with every tank shipped, warning users of its faults and what was being done to mitigate them in future production.[121] These were not just empty promises though. Twenty out of 22 serious design defects were considered resolved by mid-December 1941.[122] These fixes were applied to existing tanks through a remanufacturing programme, although it was estimated that the first 300 tanks produced could not be made battleworthy and would have to be retained in the UK for training.[123]

As with other British tanks, the Infantry Tank Mk.IV received a name in September 1941. The base model was designated Churchill I and the Infantry Tank Mk.IVA became the Churchill II.[124]

Discussion of sending these tanks to the USSR began around this time. The teething troubles the tanks were going through were not considered a major impediment, as "the Russians, good mechanics, would be able to keep them in working order and would appreciate their good fighting qualities". The weather conditions of the Eastern Front were even considered an advantage, as the tank

The main distinctive feature of the Churchill I was the 3in howitzer installed in the hull.

was prone to overheating and would hold up better in the cooler climate.[125]

Thankfully, this assumption was tested before the tanks were sent into battle. Since Russian winter could not be recreated in the mild climate of the British Isles, a decision was made in late December 1941 to send two tanks for testing in Canada.[126] Captain A. G. Sangster, a Canadian armour officer, was recalled from Great Britain for this purpose on January 17, 1942. Four crewmen and the tanks themselves departed on January 23.[127] Before his departure, Sangster studied the Churchill tank in detail at Vauxhall and forwarded an 11-page list of known defects.[128] An unofficial driver's handbook composed by Vauxhall only arrived on March 30, by which point the trials had already been completed.[129]

The Canadians deemed the tanks to be workable in winter at temperatures as low as -34° Celsius (the required -40° chill was not reached). Snow and ice packed under the tracks could immobilise the tank, but this could be resolved with aircraft deicing fluid. A system was devised to apply this fluid automatically, but an early thaw made it impossible to test its effectiveness.[130] The lifespan of the tanks was estimated to be 500 miles between major overhauls.[131] This was a problem, since although the tanks would remain in Canada, they were insufficiently reliable to use to train drivers.[132]

Meanwhile, plans to begin shipping Churchills to the USSR were well underway.

Infantry Tank Mk.IVA or Churchill II tank, Bovington Tank Museum. The BESA machine gun mounted in the hull is missing and only the shape of the firing port differentiates this tank from a Churchill I from the outside.

Soviet delegations toured factories that produced the tank in January and February 1942.[133] There were plans to begin shipments of 100 tanks of this type in March 1942,[134] but the only thing sent by then was a list of common defects, similar to the one composed by Captain Sangster.[135] The cause was twofold: one was the concern that 100 tanks were simply not enough to be a decisive force, and sending new tanks would only spoil the element of surprise.[136] The other reservation was for practical reasons. The improvements to boost the Churchill's reliability originally scheduled for January 1942 had not been introduced into production by March. Churchill tanks were heading to remanufacturing workshops straight from the factory.[137]

It took months to iron out the details of these shipments and prepare the tanks. In the meantime, the tanks kept changing. Remanufactured Churchills could be distinguished by the letter R after their WD number, fenders over the protruding tracks, and new air intakes.

Work to rid the Churchill of its design flaws didn't mean that the design stood still otherwise. The most important change made to the vehicle before the first Infantry Tank Mk.IV touched down in Europe was the introduction of a 57mm 6-pounder gun. Work on this gun began in 1938, when

Churchill III tank, Canadian War Museum. This tank was equipped with a larger welded turret and a more powerful 57mm 6-pounder gun than its predecessor. It has deep wading equipment fitted, which was not used in the Red Army.

it became clear that tanks with armour completely immune to the 40mm 2-pounder were not far beyond the horizon. Unlike the short low velocity 57mm guns of the First World War tanks, this was a potent anti-tank weapon.[138]

The small turret of the Churchill I and II tanks developed for a 2-pounder could not fit the larger 6-pounder, and so a new turret had to be developed. As it often happens in tank building, the designs had to be adapted to whatever industrial capacity was available. The Babcock and Wilcox company engaged in this project had considerable experience with welding thick plates and proposed an enlarged welded turret. There were doubts about whether or not such thick armour could be welded at all, but trials showed that the seams stood up to hits from 2-pounder and 25-pounder shot. The tank with this turret was indexed Churchill III. Seven hundred vehicles of this type were built. Since rolled plate could not be produced in sufficient quantity to meet the demand for Churchill tanks, the Churchill III was joined by the Churchill IV with a similarly shaped cast turret. 1,422 Churchill IV tanks were built, making this the most common type of Churchill tank. Early Churchill III and IV tanks still had to go through the

Churchill IV, Vadim Zadorozhniy Technical Museum. The only difference between the Churchill IV and its predecessor was the use of a cast turret instead of a welded one. PAVEL BOROVIKOV

remanufacturing programme, although the tank was beginning to find its footing.

The first Churchills to depart for the USSR were carried by the infamous convoy PQ-17. Twenty-five Churchills took the place of Matilda tanks in this convoy but due to heavy losses sustained en route, only one ship carrying the new tanks arrived at its destination. *Ocean Freedom* delivered five Churchill II and five Churchill III tanks to Arkhangelsk on July 11, 1942. A long pause in shipments followed and the next convoy to deliver Churchill tanks, PQ-18, only came on September 21, 1942. This convoy carried 15 Churchill II tanks and 59 Churchill III tanks. These were the last Churchill IIs to arrive in the USSR for a total of 20 vehicles of this type. No Churchill Is were ever sent.[139]

Convoy PQ-18 also brought Captain Cox, a Churchill tank expert. His arrival was fortunate, as the Red Army had their hands full keeping their unreliable Churchills running without the required expertise or spare parts. Despite the successes of the remanufacturing programme, nearly all Churchill tanks that came with convoy PQ-18 still had manufacturing defects. Nevertheless, orders of Churchill tanks continued. A shipment of 40 more tanks including some Churchill IVs came to

A pair of Vickers periscopes, seen here on a Cromwell tank. Even though the Red Army had encountered several tanks with these periscopes before the Churchill, it was this tank specifically that made an impression. The Vickers periscope was copied and accepted into service in the Red Army under the name MK-4, named after the tank it was copied from. PAVEL BOROVIKOV

Arkhangelsk with convoy JW-53 on January 27, 1943, and 121 tanks arrived in late February. After that, only eight more Churchills came through Vladivostok in August 1943. Shipments of Churchill III and IV tanks ceased in 1943. 344 Churchill tanks were sent in total with 253 making it to their destination, 105 of these were Churchill IVs.[140]

Trials began soon after the arrival of the first Churchills in the USSR. A tank with WD number T.31222R was chosen, but it suffered engine failure due to a bad seal. Since there were insufficient spare parts available to repair it, T.31221R was sent instead. This tank was already earmarked for the front lines, so the trials programme was abbreviated in order to spare the wear on the tank's components. In addition to the 200km the tank drove before coming to the proving grounds, it drove for 97km on paved roads and 87km on dirt roads, including special obstacle trials.

The testers did not spare the throttle. A top speed of 28kph was recorded, which was a whole 4kph faster than the official top speed. This was quite low, but the average speed on a highway was 25.4kph, not that much slower than a KV-1 tank. The tank consumed 325L of B-70 gasoline with R-9 aircraft additives per 100km of highway driving. The top speed of 17.5kph and average speed of 16.8kph on dirt roads with a fuel consumption of 382L per 100km was also not too bad.[141]

The maximum grade that the Churchill could climb depended on the terrain. The tracks lost traction in sand on slopes greater than 27°. On hills covered in grass or shrubs, the maximum slope grew to 30°, after which the tank lacked the engine power to continue.

Churchill Crocodile flamethrower tank, Patriot Park. This is one of the three tanks sent to the USSR for trials in 1945. PAVEL BOROVIKOV

Driving at a tilt was much harder for the tank, as it shed its tracks at a tilt of over 20°. The testers blamed the design of the running gear for this. Generally, the running gear gave a poor showing, with many components breaking during testing. Testers described the tank as "unfinished, both from a design and a manufacturing standpoint" due to the sheer number of defects.[142]

Observation from the tank was a mixed bag. On one hand, the range of vision afforded to the driver and his assistant was severely limited by the protruding fenders. On the other hand, the crewmen in the turret had excellent vision provided by their Vickers periscopes. The Soviets were so impressed by this design that they copied it under the index MK-4 after the designation of the tank (Infantry Tank Mk.IV). Curiously enough, the Vickers periscope was itself a copy of the Gundlach periscope that the Soviets already saw on captured Polish vehicles, but back then it did not seem to make any kind of lasting impression.[143]

The tank's gun also proved exceptional. At a range of 950m, 6-pounder shot punched through the flank of a Pz.Kpfw.III tank and came out the other side.[144] It could also penetrate the side of a Tiger tank at a similar range. The performance of the 57mm 6-pounder was similar to that of the Soviet ZIS-2, their own 57mm anti-tank gun.[145] It was found that the lack of HE shells could be overcome by firing Soviet 50mm mortar shells from the 2in bomb thrower or using HE shells delivered for American 57mm guns that were also supplied to the USSR.[146]

Despite the aforementioned drawbacks of

the design and concerns about the reliability of the engine and running gear, the report ended on a positive note: "The English heavy tank MK-IV Churchill has armament, protection, and mobility that permits it to effectively fight tanks of the German army."[147]

Churchill Crocodile

Although the Red Army had lost interest in ordering Churchill tanks by the end of 1943, the British continued to field it. Development also continued and several more types were produced. For the purposes of this book, the Churchill VII variant is of particular interest. In addition to the General Staff requirements designation A22F, this tank was also called "Churchill (Heavy)" in period documents, and for a good reason.[148] This variant had considerably thicker armour than its predecessors: up to 152mm in the front and 95mm on the sides. The hull was fully welded, which improved protection compared to earlier variants.

The cast turret had the same nominal thickness as the hull: 152mm in the front and 95mm on the sides and rear.[149] The primary armament of this tank remained the same as upgraded Churchill IV or Churchill VI tanks: a 75mm/6-pdr gun with similar ballistics to the Sherman's M3. A prototype was built in late 1943 and entered trials on January 6, 1944.[150]

The same tank showing the hull-mounted flamethrower. Testers judged this flamethrower to be better than the Soviet ATO-42. PAVEL BOROVIKOV

The flamethrower fuel was kept in a trailer. This kept the crew safe, but also reduced the tank's mobility. PAVEL BOROVIKOV

It was not the gun or the armour that piqued the interest of the Red Army. The Churchill VII was designed from the ground up with the ability to be converted into a flamethrower tank by replacing the hull machine gun with a flamethrower and attaching a trailer to carry the fuel. The converted vehicle was called Churchill Crocodile.

The Red Army, an avid user of flamethrower tanks since the early 1930s, was a prime customer for this new tank, but there was not a lot of effort made to market it to them. The first mention of the Churchill Crocodile in GBTU's internal correspondence dates to March 1945. A decision was made to order three tanks. Churchill Crocodiles with WD numbers T.252466/K, T.2524688/K and T.252469/K (the letter K indicated that this was a flamethrower tank), which were shipped to the USSR for testing with convoy JW-66.

Trials revealed that this was truly an exceptional flamethrower tank. The storage of fuel in a trailer and use of compressed nitrogen as a propellant considerably improved the safety of the crew. The position of the flamethrower in the hull allowed the crew to fire the main gun and flamethrower at the same time. The flamethrower had an effective range of 100m and a maximum range of 120m in part due to a very effective composition of the flamethrower fuel.

An ATO-42 flamethrower installed in a T-O34 flamethrower tank tested in parallel had an effective range of 100-110m and a maximum range of 126m with Soviet fuel, but with British fuel the range increased to 145m. When filled with Soviet fuel, the

Churchill Crocodile's range dropped to 90m. Despite the T-O34's slight edge in range, Soviet testers gave the Churchill Crocodile's flamethrower a higher grade due to a larger amount of fuel fired per shot and greater overall fuel capacity.

In general, the Churchill Crocodile was considered worse than the Soviet tank. In part, this was due to the fuel trailer. Even though it protected the crew, it made any kind of manoeuvres (especially turning or reversing) more difficult for the driver.[151] Of the three Churchill Crocodile tanks sent to the USSR, only T.252468/K survives to this day. It can be seen on display at the Patriot Park museum.

Battle of Stalingrad

Churchill tanks were considered to be on par with the Soviet KV-1 and KV-1S tanks, and thus received the honour of being sent exclusively to Guards Heavy Tank Breakthrough Regiments formed according to TO&E 010/267. Due to the small number of Churchills received, there were very few of these units. The first wave of regiments armed with Churchill tanks consisted of the 47th, 48th, 49th, and 50th Guards Heavy Tank Breakthrough Regiments. The 50th regiment received 19 out of the 20 Churchill II tanks sent to the USSR and two Churchill III tanks. The last Churchill II went to the 194th Training Tank Brigade.

The regiments were officially formed on October 8, 1942, but Churchill tanks exhibited a high number of technical issues which considerably delayed their debut in battle. The first Red Army unit armed with Churchill tanks to be ready for combat was the 48th Gds. HTR. The regiment was allocated to the Don Front on December 31, 1942, in order to take part in the final stages of the Battle of Stalingrad.[152]

The regiment disembarked at the Kachalino railway station on January 20, 1943, with 21 Churchills on hand. The tanks were needed in action urgently and went into battle on the very next day in support of the 216th Guards Rifle Regiment of the 51st Guards Rifle Division.[153]

The 51st Guards Rifle Division was tasked with taking the Gonchara homestead and advancing in the direction of the Gumrak airstrip, but had no luck due to powerful artillery and machine gun fire.[154] The arrival of Churchill tanks made a noticeable difference. After three days of fruitless attempts to move forward, the infantry attacked once more at 11am on January 21 and successfully captured the homestead by 3pm.[155] This success came at a cost with two Churchill tanks burned up and three more knocked out.[156]

The tanks and infantry continued to move in the direction of Gumrak, reaching its outskirts by the evening of January 23.[157] The airstrip was surrounded by 2km of open steppe, a deathtrap for infantry, but perfect terrain for the Churchill's thick armour. An attack began at 7.30am and by 8.30am the airstrip was in Soviet hands.[158] Even though it was still early in the day, there was no rush to continue the attack towards the Krasniy Oktyabr settlement, the 51st Guards' next target. The infantry needed rest and with only seven functional tanks remaining the 48th Guards Heavy Tank Breakthrough Regiment could not operate on its own.[159]

German resistance around Stalingrad began to collapse. The 51st Guards Rifle Division and 48th Guards Heavy Tank Breakthrough Regiment were ordered to link up with the 62nd Army, cutting the German garrison in half. The 48th Guards continued to support the infantry in city fighting until the end of January, when it returned to Gumrak to repair and refit. On February 1, the battered regiment was withdrawn into the

Path of the 48th Guards Heavy Tank Breakthrough Regiment fighting in support of the 51st Guards Rifle Division in late January 1943. This was a brief but fierce battle to break through the German defences around Stalingrad and destroy the forces remaining in the city.

- River
- Cities and towns
- - - Front line January 16th
- ——— Front line January 22nd
- → 48th Guards Jan 21–Jan 30

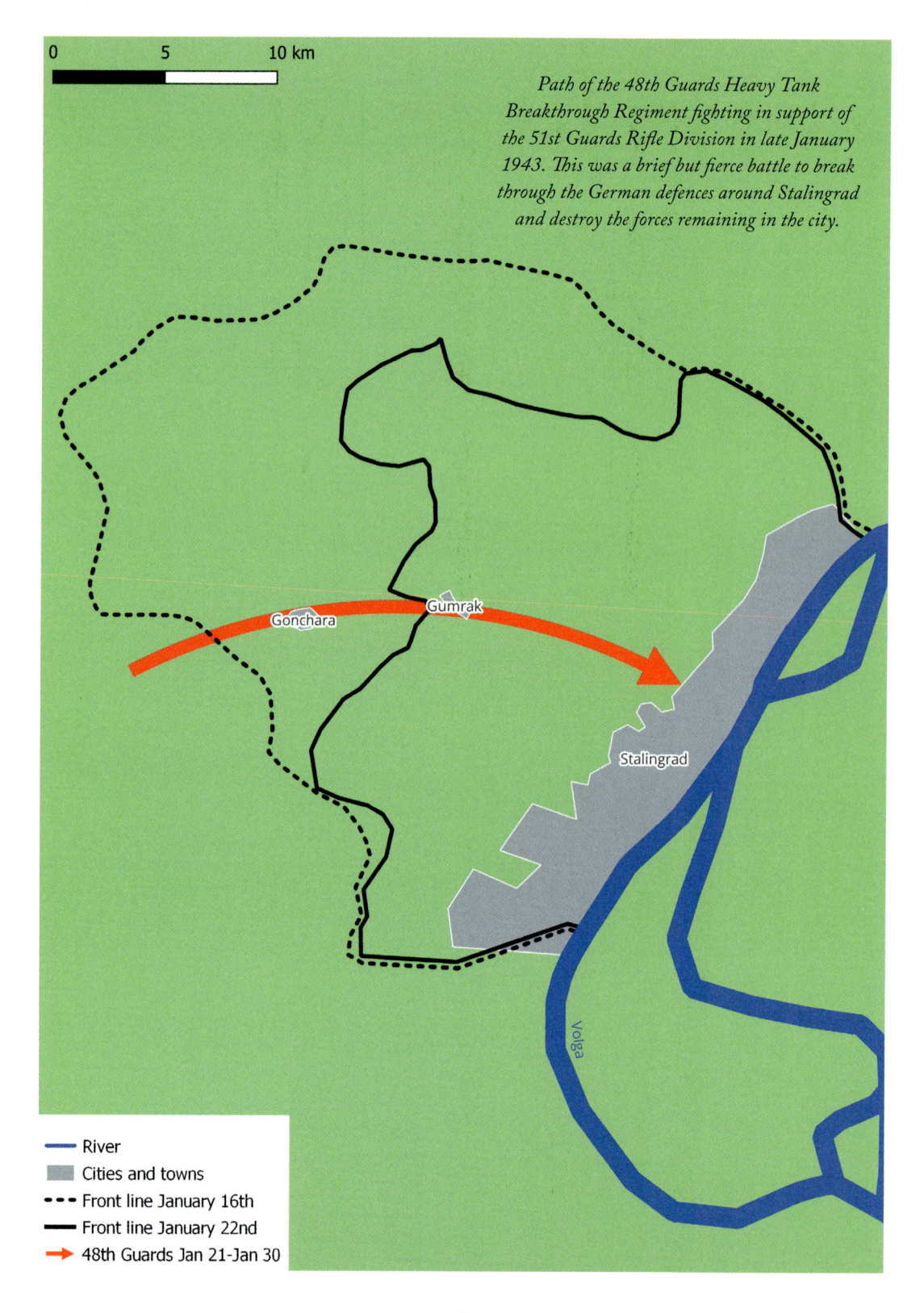

40-Tonner J Pz Kpfw **Mk IV** (Churchill III)

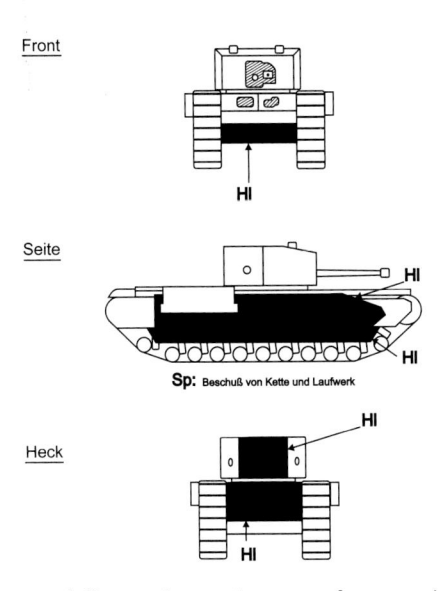

Front

Seite

Sp: Beschuß von Kette und Laufwerk

Heck

A German instruction manual on engaging a Churchill III tank with a 7.5cm KwK L/24. Black areas indicate places where the main armour can be penetrated, hashed areas indicate places that can be hit to damage components without penetrating the tank's armour. The Churchill was vulnerable to HEAT (Hl) ammunition, but if that was not available the gunner's only option was to fire high explosive (Sp) at the tank's tracks and running gear.

40-Tonner J Pz Kpfw **Mk IV** (Churchill III)

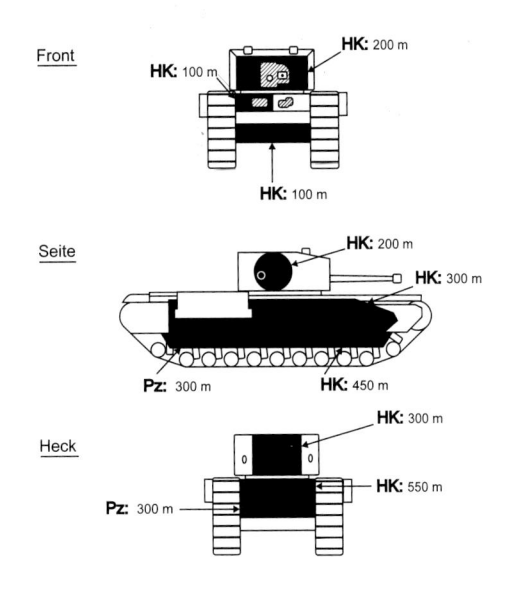

Front — HK: 200 m, HK: 100 m, HK: 100 m

Seite — HK: 200 m, HK: 300 m, Pz: 300 m, HK: 450 m

Heck — HK: 300 m, HK: 550 m, Pz: 300 m

A German instruction manual on engaging a Churchill III tank with a 5cm KwK 40. The front armour could only be penetrated at close range with tungsten carbide shot (HK). The sides and rear were vulnerable to regular armour piercing shells (Pz), but only at close range. The Churchill was very well protected against early war German tanks and anti-tank guns.

Front's reserve.[160] The last German forces in the city surrendered on the very next day. The Battle of Stalingrad was over.[161]

The 48th Gds HTR was bloodied, but in better condition than one might expect after more than a week of continuous attacks. Only three tanks were total losses. Seven more were knocked out and required major repairs. Nine tanks were knocked out and required medium repairs, seven of which had already been repaired previously.[162]

Despite the rush to put the tanks into action, the Chief of Staff of Armoured and Motorized Forces of the 6th Guards Army Lt Colonel Zhagulo described the cooperation between tanks, infantry, and artillery as well organised. There were no issues with supplying the tanks. The tanks themselves did their job, although Zhagulo states that there were losses due to design defects and the fact that the Churchill was not designed for winter warfare. Tank losses due to breakdowns were compounded by a lack of repair personnel who had experience with these kinds of tanks. Nevertheless, the overall impression was positive.[163] Five

Churchill tank drivers, two radio operators, and two gunners were awarded the For Courage medal for this battle and one gunner and two drivers received the For Battle Merit medal.[164]

Battle of Kursk

The 48th Guards Heavy Tank Breakthrough Regiment continued to fight through the spring of 1943. Thanks to another batch of 150 Churchill tanks that arrived from Great Britain, the regiment could be refilled to authorised strength in time for its next great challenge: the Battle of Kursk. The 48th Gds HTR met the start of the battle with a full complement of 21 Churchill tanks, three loads of 57mm ammunition, three loads of machine gun ammunition, and two loads of gasoline.[165] The tanks were stationed some 50km north of Belgorod.[166] The 5th Guards Tank Corps that the regiment was attached to was stationed in the second echelon of defence in order to counter enemy breakthroughs. It didn't need to wait to see action, as it was soon reported that two German tank divisions penetrated Soviet defences at 2.30pm on July 5 and were moving north towards Gremuchiy. The 5th Guards Tank Corps was ordered to stop the enemy and push them back with a counterattack. The tanks moved out at 8pm, with the Churchills accompanying the corps artillery to Luchki.[167]

The 5th Gds TC received new orders at noon on the next day. Its tanks were to counterattack enemy forces advancing towards Yablochki. The Corps allocated a considerable force to this endeavour: the regiment of Churchill tanks was joined by the 21st Guards Tank Brigade (44 T-34, 21 T-70) and 22nd Guards Tank Brigade (49 T-34, 21 T-70). The 20th Guards Tank Brigade (32 T-34, 28 T-70) was also sent, but did not arrive in time.[168]

Documents of the 48th Gds HTR also only mention assistance from the 21st Gds TBr.[169] Nevertheless, the arrival of a large number of tanks gave the enemy pause. Rather than attacking head on, the Germans opted to seek a weakness in Soviet lines, striking at the newly arrived 6th Guards Motorized Rifle Brigade on the left flank before they had a chance to dig in. The 1st Tank Army on the right flank of the 5th Gds TC also offered little resistance. Under threat of encirclement, the tankers held out until midnight and then withdrew north to Prokhorovka and Belenikhino.

This day cost the 5th Gds TC 110 tanks. In return, the Soviet tankers claimed 95 enemy tanks and 30 SPGs destroyed.[170] The Churchills claimed a considerable portion of the victories (23 tanks and 13 SPGs), reporting seven losses of their own in combat in addition to one tank destroyed by bombs during travel. Seven more tanks were knocked out during the withdrawal early in the morning of July 7. Out of six remaining Churchills, five were damaged. The functional Churchill was transferred to the 21st Gds TBr immediately and the five remaining tanks were transferred after repairs were completed on July 9.[171] Five of these tanks were still in service by July 11. Three were lost on July 12, two of them hit by bombs. No Churchill tanks were left in the 5th Guards Tank Corps by July 20.[172]

There was another unit of Churchill tanks not too far away: the 36th Guards Heavy Tank Breakthrough Regiment attached to the 18th Tank Corps. The corps was located at Rossosh, 130km east of Belgorod, when the Battle of Kursk began. By July 9, the corps moved north of Prokhorovka, gathering at Malaya Psinka.[173] Nineteen Churchill tanks out of the regiment's 21 were still in service at this point.[174]

The 18th TC went into action on July 12,

BRITISH INFANTRY TANKS IN SOVIET SERVICE

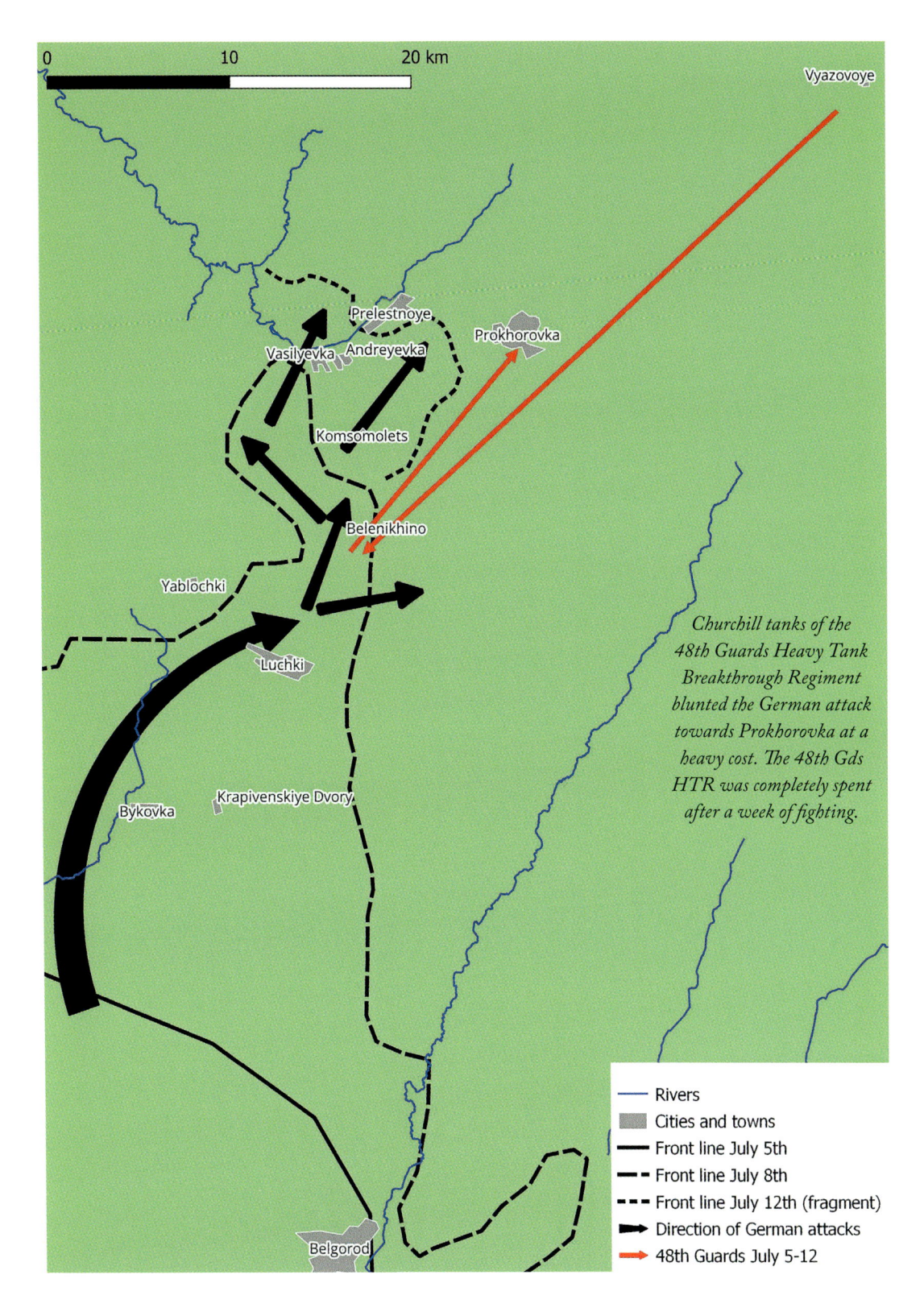

Churchill tanks of the 48th Guards Heavy Tank Breakthrough Regiment blunted the German attack towards Prokhorovka at a heavy cost. The 48th Gds HTR was completely spent after a week of fighting.

——	Rivers
▓	Cities and towns
——	Front line July 5th
– – –	Front line July 8th
····	Front line July 12th (fragment)
➡	Direction of German attacks
➡	48th Guards July 5-12

BRITISH TANKS OF THE RED ARMY

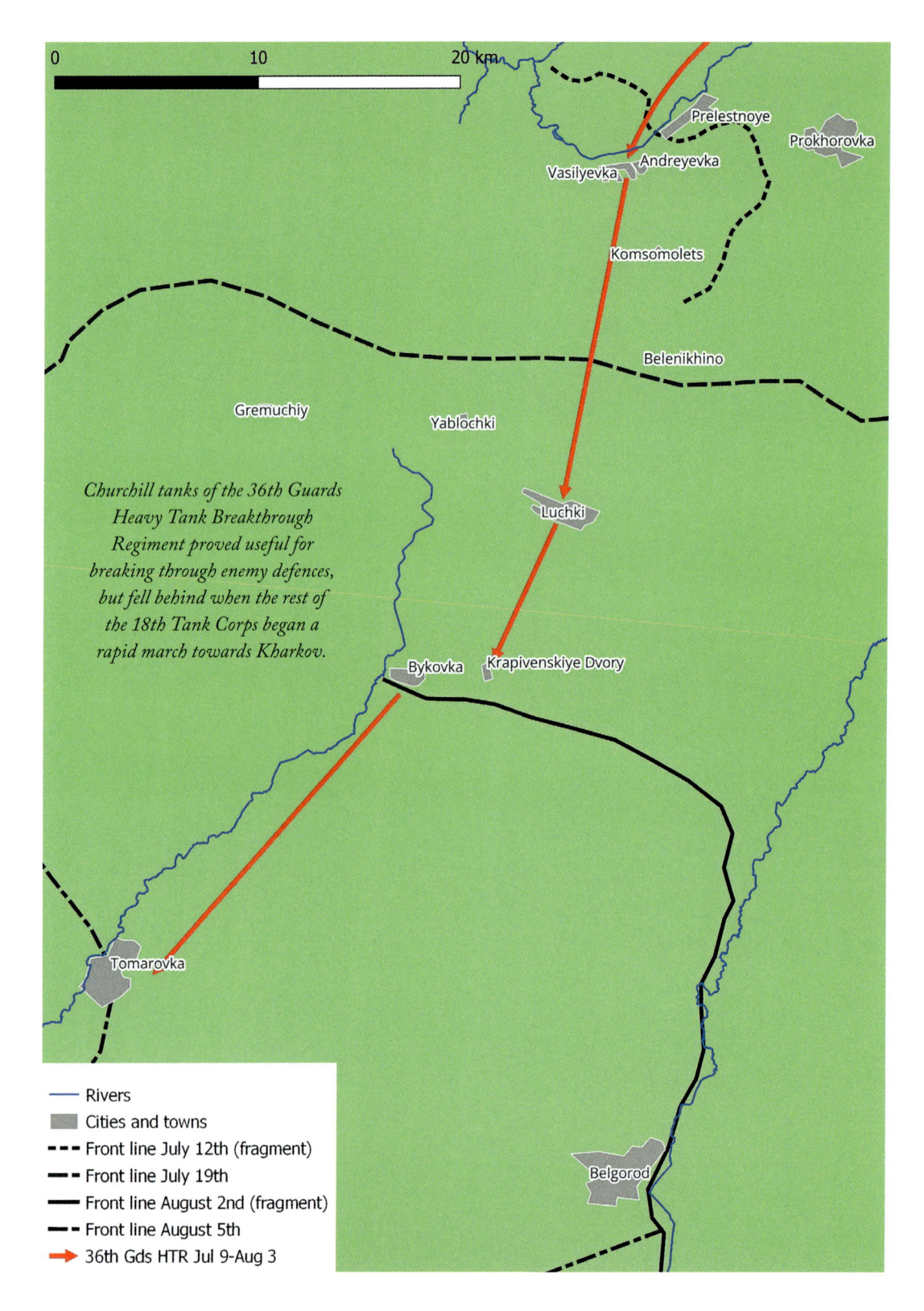

Churchill tanks of the 36th Guards Heavy Tank Breakthrough Regiment proved useful for breaking through enemy defences, but fell behind when the rest of the 18th Tank Corps began a rapid march towards Kharkov.

Prelestnoye
Prokhorovka
Vasilyevka
Andreyevka
Komsomolets
Belenikhino
Gremuchiy
Yablochki
Luchki
Bykovka
Krapivenskiye Dvory
Tomarovka
Belgorod

Legend:
— Rivers
■ Cities and towns
--- Front line July 12th (fragment)
–– Front line July 19th
— Front line August 2nd (fragment)
-- Front line August 5th
→ 36th Gds HTR Jul 9–Aug 3

1943. The commander of the 5th Guards Tank Army ordered the 18th and 29th TC to attack south in order to break the enemy defences at Andreevka-Komsomolets and clear the way for the Army to attack southwards. The 170th and 181st Tank Brigades were in the first echelon of the attack. The Churchills of the 36th Gds HTR were assigned to the right flank of the second echelon.[175]

The attack began at 8.30am. The corps progressed slowly, as the uneven terrain made manoeuvring with tanks difficult. A lack of air cover meant that serious damage was taken due to enemy bombers. The attack was not entirely successful either. At the end of the day, the commander of the 18th TC ordered his units to dig in at the Vasilyevka-Prelestnoye line in order to avoid a pointless attack into well-prepared enemy defences.[176]

Even though the Churchills were advancing in the second echelon on the flank where German defences were weaker, they took most of the damage. Eleven Churchill tanks were lost or damaged that day compared to just six T-34s and four T-70s.[177] Six of those Churchills burned up.[178] On the other hand, losses in personnel among Churchill crews were minimal: six men killed and 15 wounded.[179] The 36th Gds HTR claimed six enemy tanks destroyed that day including two Tigers.[180]

The 18th TC held its positions over the next two days, deflecting enemy counterattacks.[181] By July 16, the 36th Gds HTR had only nine Churchill tanks in service out of the 19 it had at the start of the battle. One required medium repairs and two more major repairs. Seven were lost irreparably. The regiment's maintenance personnel had been hard at work keeping the tanks running, having completed 25 minor repairs and two medium repairs.[182] The regiment was still reporting three loads of ammunition but only 1.7 loads of fuel, suggesting that they did a lot of driving but not a lot of fighting since the operation began.[183]

July 17 marked a lull in the fighting as both sides strengthened their defences.[184] Another Churchill returned to service, increasing the number of functional tanks to 10. Two more tanks that were previously knocked out were recovered that day. The 36th Gds HTR successfully deflected an enemy attack on July 17 with no losses.[185]

The 5th Guards Tank Army decided to take another crack at the German defences. The 18th Tank Corps received an order to attack towards Belgorod at 4pm on July 18. The 36th Gds HTR would once again be in the second echelon on the right flank with orders to attack towards Bykovka and Krapivenskiye Dvory once the corps passed Luchki. This time, the 5th Gds TA had better luck and the enemy's defences began to crumble.

The 18th TC faced resistance, but a lack of dense minefields and artificial obstacles suggested that the Germans were not prepared for this attack.[186] One Churchill tank did end up hitting a mine, but another was repaired in time to take its place.[187] At the cost of another Churchill, the 36th Gds HTR pushed to Luchki by July 21[188] and finally reached Krapivenskiye Dvory on July 23.[189] The grinding offensive took a heavy toll on the 18th TC and it was ordered to hand off its positions to the 42nd Guards Rifle Division on July 24 and retreat in order to refit.[190]

Repairs were progressing slowly with only eight Churchills ready for action and two more tanks undergoing repairs by July 27.[191] One of the disabled tanks took a hit to the turret that deformed the armour and limited the turret traverse, the other had engine trouble.[192] Both problems were classified as major repairs.[193]

40-Tonner J Pz Kpfw **Mk IV** (Churchill III)

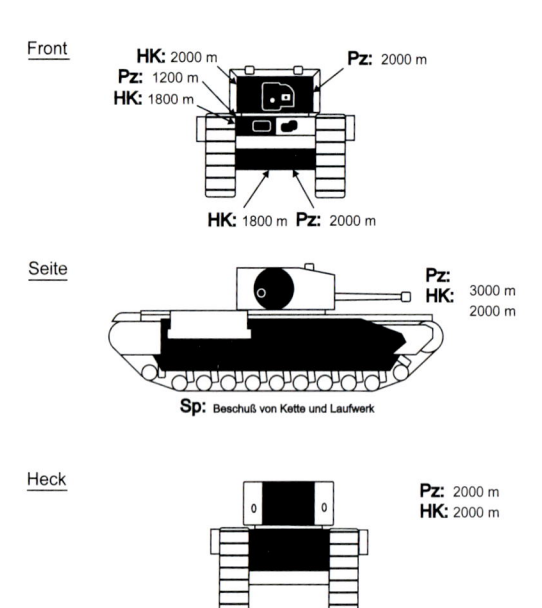

A German instruction manual on engaging a Churchill III tank with a 7.5cm KwK 42 mounted on the Panther tank. Black areas indicate places where the main armour can be penetrated. The Churchill's armour could be penetrated at long range using either armour piercing shells (Pz) or tungsten core shot (HK). High explosive shells (Sp) could also destroy the tank's tracks and running gear.

The repairs had not been completed by the time the 18th TC received new orders. With enemy defences weakened, the Corps was needed to exploit a breakthrough. Eight Churchills, 85 T-34s, and 14 T-70s were assembled around Bykovka by midnight of August 3 in order to support the 33rd Rifle Corps in its mission to cut off the Belgorod-Tomarovka highway.[194] The 18th Tank Corps attacked in a wedge formation with the bloodied 36th Gds HTR alone in the second echelon.[195] Even without being involved in combat on August 3, one Churchill fell behind due to mechanical problems.[196] The seven remaining Churchills pursued the retreating enemy over the course of the next few days as the 18th TC advanced towards Kharkov.[197] Only three Churchills were still running by August 8 with four more undergoing repairs.[198]

Another Churchill broke down on the following day.[199] All Churchills of the 36th Gds HTR were in need of repairs by August 10.[200] Still limping along behind the 18th TC, the tanks were in rough shape. The three Churchills that could still drive were in need of medium repairs. Nine more tanks listed in the regiment's inventory needed major repairs.[201] The heavy infantry tank proved unsuitable for the sustained marches required to pursue a fleeing enemy.

Leningrad and Pskov Offensives

The depleted 36th Guards Heavy Tank Breakthrough Regiment was down after the Battle of Kursk, but not out. The trickle of Churchill tanks arriving towards the end of 1943 was enough to rebuild the regiment at least partially. The replenished unit was attached to the 67th Army on February 13, 1944.[202] At the time, the 67th Army was taking part in the offensive aimed at lifting the blockade around Leningrad that had gripped the city since 1941.[203] The blockade was already lifted by the time the Churchill tanks showed up, but the fighting was far from over. The Germans still possessed considerable forces in the north, and the combination of a network of fortifications built over the course of two and a half years and difficult terrain that favoured the defender made this a tough nut to crack. On February 1, 1944, the 67th Army was ordered to attack towards Luga and destroy the enemy forces holding the city and its surroundings[204] and then proceed to Pskov.[205]

The 36th Guards Heavy Tank Breakthrough Regiment arrived too late for the liberation of Leningrad and Luga, its Churchill tanks limping 40km behind the front lines of the 67th Army for the second half of February 1944.

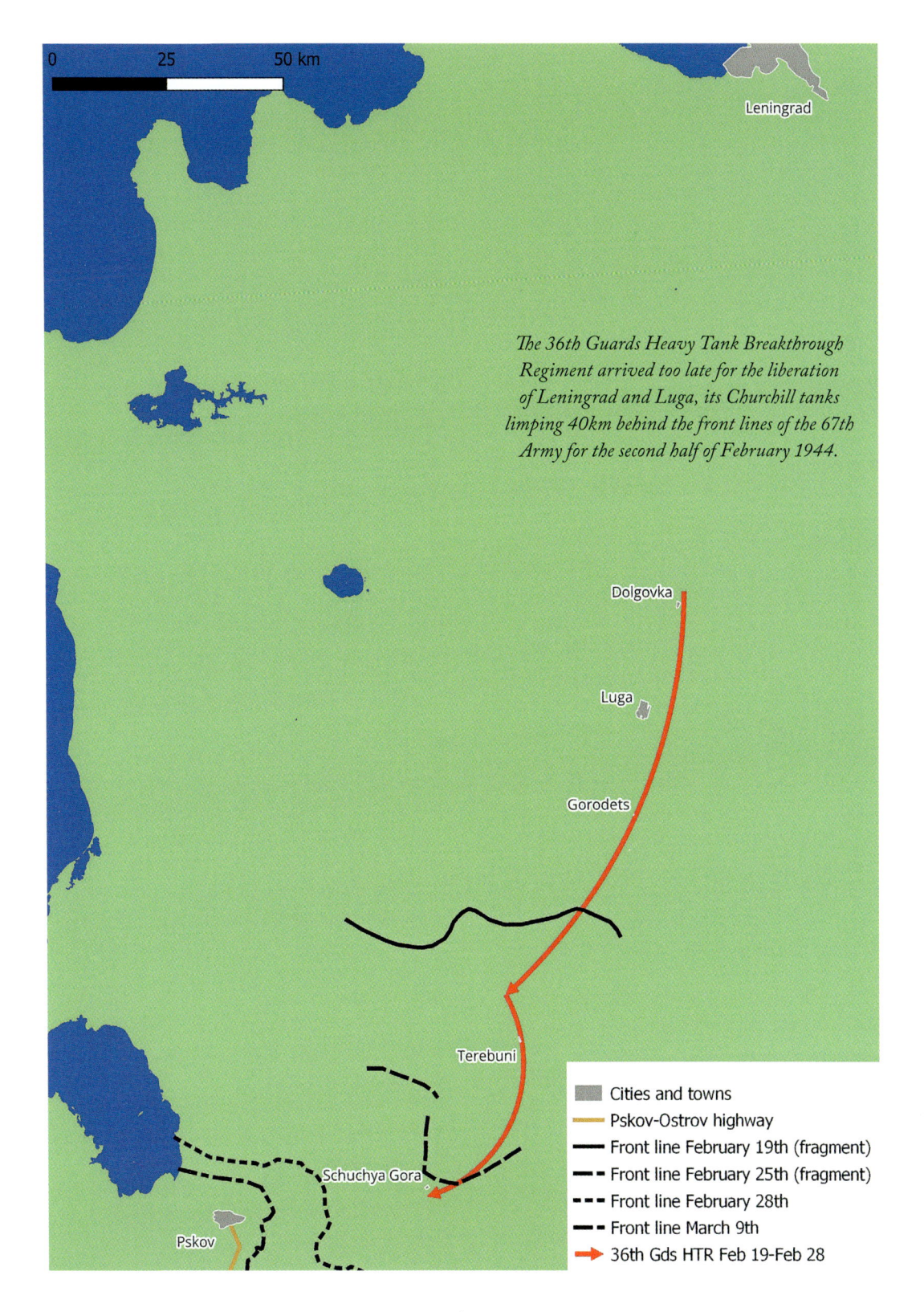

The Churchills were set to arrive just as elements of the 67th Army liberated Luga,[206] and thus did not take part in this battle. However, the tanks did not arrive as scheduled anyway. The entry for the 36th Guards Heavy Tank Breakthrough Regiment in the log of the Chief of Staff for Armoured and Mechanized Forces of the 67th Army for February 13 simply reads: "The 36th Gds HTR has not arrived as of 13.02".[207]

The note for the following day was not any more encouraging. Elements of the unit had arrived at Dolgovka, but a considerable number of vehicles fell behind. The Commander of Armoured and Mechanized Forces of the 67th Army allocated February 14 and 15 for the regiment to pull up its tanks and perform necessary maintenance and repairs. The unit reported 14 functional Churchill and two Valentine IX tanks in its inventory.[208] The number of working Churchills went up to 17 by February 16.[209]

Repairs continued on the following day[210] and the 36th Gds HTR only set out towards Gorodets on February 19, losing two of its Churchills to technical problems on the way.[211] Rather than fighting, the regiment followed the main forces of the 67th Army, chiefly preoccupied with finding a route suitable for its heavy tanks.[212] The Churchills were lagging a distance of some 40km behind the front lines by the end of February.[213] It's no wonder that the summary report on the actions of the 67th Army in February laconically described the performance of its tanks in just one sentence: "Tank forces were not used in battle".[214]

The advance of the 67th Army slowed down as it approached the heavy enemy defences around Pskov. The 36th Gds HTR caught up with its superiors on March 2 and was attached to the 65th Rifle Division of the 7th Rifle Corps.[215] By this point, there were only 14 Churchill tanks left.[216] Two more broke down on the next day.[217] There was not much time to put them back in action, as the 67th Army was ordered to breach the enemy's defences by March 10.[218]

The 7th Rifle Corps was attacking from the south with the objective to take the Pskov-Ostrov highway.[219] The tanks were not used in the probing attacks undertaken on March 4-8 and there was time to repair one Churchill tank for a total of 13 Churchills and two Valentines ready for action.[220]

The Churchill tanks finally saw battle on March 9, supporting the 65th Rifle Division and 401st Self Propelled Artillery Regiment in their attack towards Yudino.[221] In particular, Churchill tanks supporting the 60th Rifle Regiment achieved some success near Bayevo,[222] breaking through minefields and wire obstacles. Further progress was impossible, as the supporting infantry was suppressed by machine gun fire.[223] Without an infantry escort, the tanks were forced to turn back.

The situation repeated itself on March 10. Even though the tanks managed to fight their way across an anti-tank ditch at Zuyevo, the infantry could not support their advance.[224] The 36th Gds HTR was down to five Churchills and just one Valentine by the end of March 10. Six tanks were destroyed by artillery fire and burned up, two more were damaged by artillery, and one tank was lost to mines.[225] Another four were lost on March 11 during an attack on Lekhino. There was little to show for these losses; the regiment claimed seven enemy guns, 11 mortars, and five machine guns destroyed as well as up to 175 enemy soldiers killed.[226]

Rather than smashing its breakthrough tanks against enemy defences in vain, the 67th Army concentrated its remaining armour. The 401st SPG Regiment, 36th Gds HTR, and remaining tanks from the 40th Tank Regiment were reassigned to support

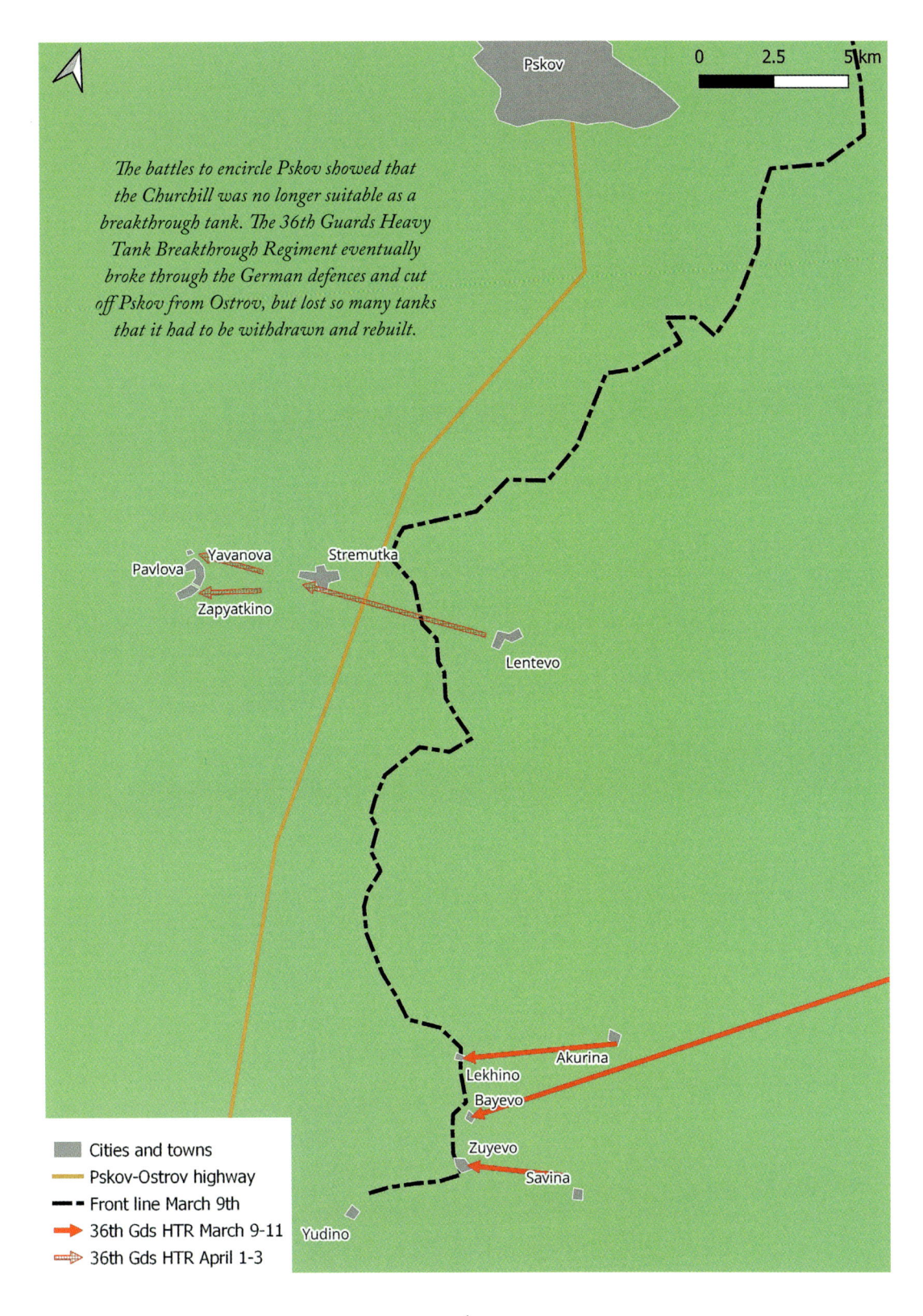

The battles to encircle Pskov showed that the Churchill was no longer suitable as a breakthrough tank. The 36th Guards Heavy Tank Breakthrough Regiment eventually broke through the German defences and cut off Pskov from Ostrov, but lost so many tanks that it had to be withdrawn and rebuilt.

Legend:
- Cities and towns
- Pskov-Ostrov highway
- Front line March 9th
- 36th Gds HTR March 9-11
- 36th Gds HTR April 1-3

the 511th Rifle Regiment of the 239th Rifle Division in another attempt to take Lekhino.[227] Before this could be done, the tankers had a pause from March 13-17 to rest and repair their damaged vehicles.[228] This was not enough for the heavily beaten 36th Gds HTR and only four tanks were in action by March 17.[229]

It was clear that the enemy's defences around Pskov would not be easy to crack. A pause followed as the opposing forces limited themselves to reconnaissance and harassing artillery fire.[230] Armoured units continued to recover their disabled vehicles.[231] Some vehicles were shuffled around the 67th Army's tank units. The 36th Gds HTR gave up their Valentines to the 40th Tank Regiment, receiving four SU-152 SPGs from the 1536th Heavy SPG Regiment.[232]

The 67th Army renewed its offensive on April 1, with the revitalised 36th Gds HTR supporting the 314th Rifle Regiment of the 46th Rifle Division with its six Churchills and four SU-152s.[233] This attack finally seized the Pskov-Ostrov highway near Stremutka,[234] but this was once again a very costly move for the heavy tanks. The 36th Guards was down to four Churchills and two SU-152s by the end of April 1[235] and two Churchills and one SU-152 by the end of April 2.[236] By April 4 the 36th Gds HTR was pulled out of combat and tasked with recovering its lost vehicles. Still-running tanks and SPGs were transferred to the 1902nd SPG Regiment[237] and 31st Guards Heavy Tank Regiment.[238] On April 12, the regiment was pulled out of the reserve of the Leningrad Front in order to refit. It was rebuilt in June 1944, this time with IS-2 tanks rather than Churchills.[239]

The battles around Pskov in the spring of 1944 were the last in which heavy tank regiments fully armed with Churchill tanks were used. The Churchill's armour and armament were comparable with those of the KV-1 and KV-1S tank, but those were already considered inadequate by the Red Army by the spring of 1943.

The tank's poor reliability could be forgiven when its armour and firepower made it a force to be reckoned with on the battlefield, but its shortcomings seemed more and more apparent as the power of German anti-tank artillery grew. The Churchill couldn't measure up to the newly arriving IS-2 tanks in armament, armour, mobility or reliability. That is not to say that Churchill tanks disappeared from the front lines overnight. Handfuls of Churchills appeared here and there throughout 1944, although they were no longer exclusively used by Guards Heavy Tank Regiments.

The 260th Guards Heavy Tank Breakthrough Regiment equipped with 32 KV tanks and six Churchills fought at Vyborg in June 1944. There were also three Churchill tanks used by the 39th Tank Regiment attached to the 38th Army, 1st Ukrainian Front in March 1944 and 10 Churchills in the 82nd Tank Regiment of the 8th Army, Leningrad Front in September 1944.[240]

The tank was considered obsolete by 1945.[241] Nine Churchills were lost between January 1 and May 9, 1945, with only three tanks of this type remaining in front line units by the end of the Great Patriotic War.[242] No Churchill II, III, or IV tanks used by the Red Army survive today.

Churchill tanks currently on display in Russian museums are either examples of the Churchill VII Crocodile, that was never used in combat, or foreign Churchills purchased by private collectors in recent years.[243]

II.
Matilda and Valentine Tanks in Combat

CHURCHILL TANKS were used as a part of Guards Heavy Tank Regiments, which makes it easy to track their combat career separately. See the chapter titled Churchill Tanks in Combat for a service history of this vehicle in the ranks of the Red Army. Conversely, Matilda and Valentine tanks were used in ordinary Tank Brigades, Independent Tank Battalions, and Tank Regiments, both Guards and otherwise, either on their own or mixed with Soviet tanks of various types.

As more than 4,000 vehicles of this type arrived in the USSR, it is impossible to cover the history of every British tank in the ranks of the Red Army. Instead, this book will focus on key battles of the Second World War where British tanks made a considerable contribution and give the reader an idea of how the Matilda and Valentine performed throughout the Great Patriotic War and Soviet-Japanese War.

Battle of Moscow

Even though Operation Barbarossa failed to achieve its objectives in the summer of 1941, the Germans were far from beaten. Operation Typhoon launched just as the first British tanks and support personnel were arriving in the USSR. With Soviet tank production at its lowest as tank factories were evacuating, a race was on to get these tanks to the front lines during this pivotal moment in the war.

The training centre in Kazan had been set up and 120 crews had completed an accelerated training course by mid-November 1941 as the Germans neared Moscow. Even though a month of training on British tanks was less than ideal, they were urgently needed on the front lines. The tankers were formed into battalions, each nominally containing 24 vehicles: 21 Matildas and three T-60s (TO&E #010/395). In practice, the composition could be quite different.

Three tank battalions (137th, 138th, 139th) armed with British tanks were formed and collected into the 146th Independent Tank Brigade led by Lieutenant Colonel I. I. Sergeev. The 138th Tank Battalion was not equipped in time, but by November 20 the brigade had the 137th and 139th Tank Battalions in its ranks with 21 Valentine II and 10 T-60 tanks each.[244]

The tankers received their orders at 4am on November 20. The 146th TBr was sent to protect the retreating 78th Rifle Division. Heading out on November 21, the brigade established positions east of Istra, straddling the Volokolamsk highway. The infantry that they were supposed to help was nowhere to be found. Contact was only established by 10pm. It turned out that the situation was quite serious, as the 78th RD was partially encircled. A company of Valentine tanks (called "Valentina" in the brigade's documents) was dispatched to help them escape. Two Valentine tanks were lost in battle, with the brigade's documents remarking that the real cause of the losses was a lack of cooperation from the infantry.[245]

This was just the beginning of a string of events which showed that the Red Army still had much to learn about combined arms warfare. The 139th Tank Battalion was extracted from the 146th TBr on November 23 on the orders of Lieutenant General Rokossovsky, commander of the 16th Army. This sapped the striking power of the brigade considerably. The battalion was only replaced on December 8 by the 55th Independent Tank Battalion with T-34 and T-60 tanks, but with "quite worn materiel and, unlike in other units, quite undisciplined personnel".[246]

Infantry and combined arms commanders continued to let the tankers down. On November 23, the tanks were positioned in three anti-tank belts to shore up the front line, but the commander of the nearby 108th Rifle Division requisitioned three tanks for an attack against German positions in Lukino.

The attack was a disaster. Organisation was poor and no infantry support was arranged. The tanks turned back once they realised they were alone, but the infantry commander sent them back into battle without organising due support. One of the three tanks was knocked out and another was damaged.[247]

The brigade attacked Stepankovo on November 26, 1941, and successfully retook the village from the Germans despite a complete absence of support from its own infantry. On November 28, the village had to be abandoned. The 1308th Rifle Regiment was sent to defend Yeremeevo alongside the 146th TBr, but retreated at the first sight of

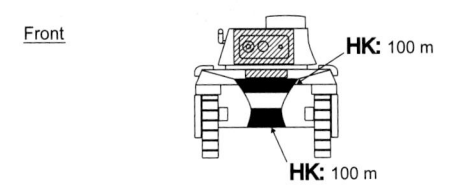

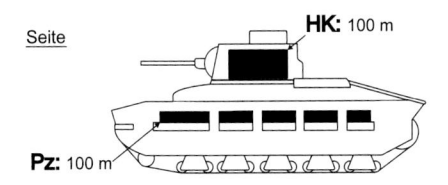

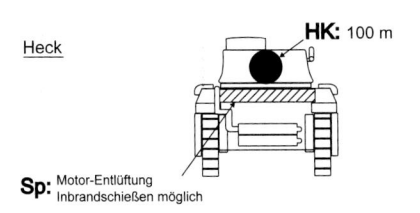

26-Tonner m.J. Pz Kpfw **Mk II** (Matilda II)

Front
HK: 100 m
HK: 100 m

Seite
HK: 100 m
Pz: 100 m

Heck
HK: 100 m

Sp: Motor-Entlüftung
Inbrandschießen möglich

16-Tonner J. Pz Kpfw **Mk III** (Valentine)

Front
HK: 150 m
HK: 150 m

Seite
HK: 150 m
HK: 150 m

Heck
HK: 150 m
HK: 150 m

Sp: Motor-Entlüftung
Inbrandschießen möglich

A German instruction manual on engaging a Matilda tank with a 3.7cm Pak. Black areas indicate places where the main armour can be penetrated, hashed areas indicate places that can be hit to damage components without penetrating the tank's armour.

The Matilda was only vulnerable at very close range if tungsten carbide shot (HK) was used. With regular armour piercing shells (Pz), the German gunner only had hopes of hitting the tank in the side through the slits in the spaced armour. From the rear, the engine could be set on fire with a lucky shot through the cooling system grilles on the engine deck.

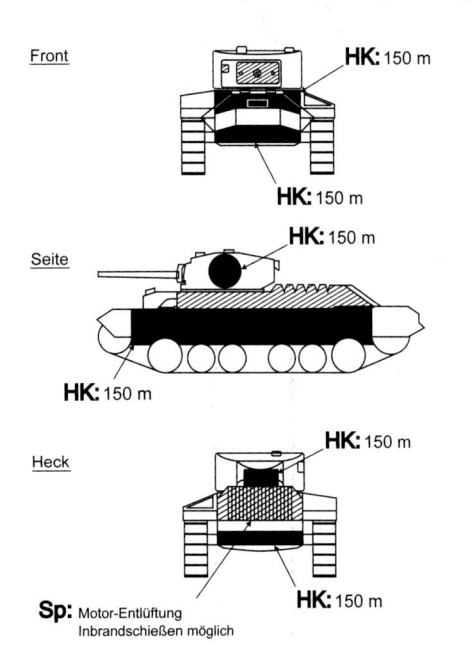

Just like the Matilda, the Valentine was very difficult to destroy with a 37mm anti-tank gun. The German gunners' only options were tungsten carbide shot at close range or firing at the rear in hopes of setting fire to the engine.

German tanks. The brigade had to hold the village using only its own motorised riflemen. This was a relatively small force that could only hold a narrow section of the front line, and the brigade was encircled and had to break out.[248]

Back in Kazan, the 138th Independent Tank Battalion received its materiel soon after its brethren had departed for the front line. Its lineup was a little more diverse: 15 Matildas, six Valentines, and 10 T-60s. The battalion was attached to the 7th Guards Rifle Division on November 26.

On the same day, it took up positions north-west of Zelenograd together with the division's 159th Rifle Regiment and 219th Howitzer Artillery Regiment. The fighting in this sector was fierce, characterised by constant attacks and counterattacks from both sides. Between November 27 and 29 the infantry lost 202 riflemen killed and 355 wounded. Unfortunately, neither the tank regiment nor its superior division appear to have left any detailed impressions of the tanks' performance.[249]

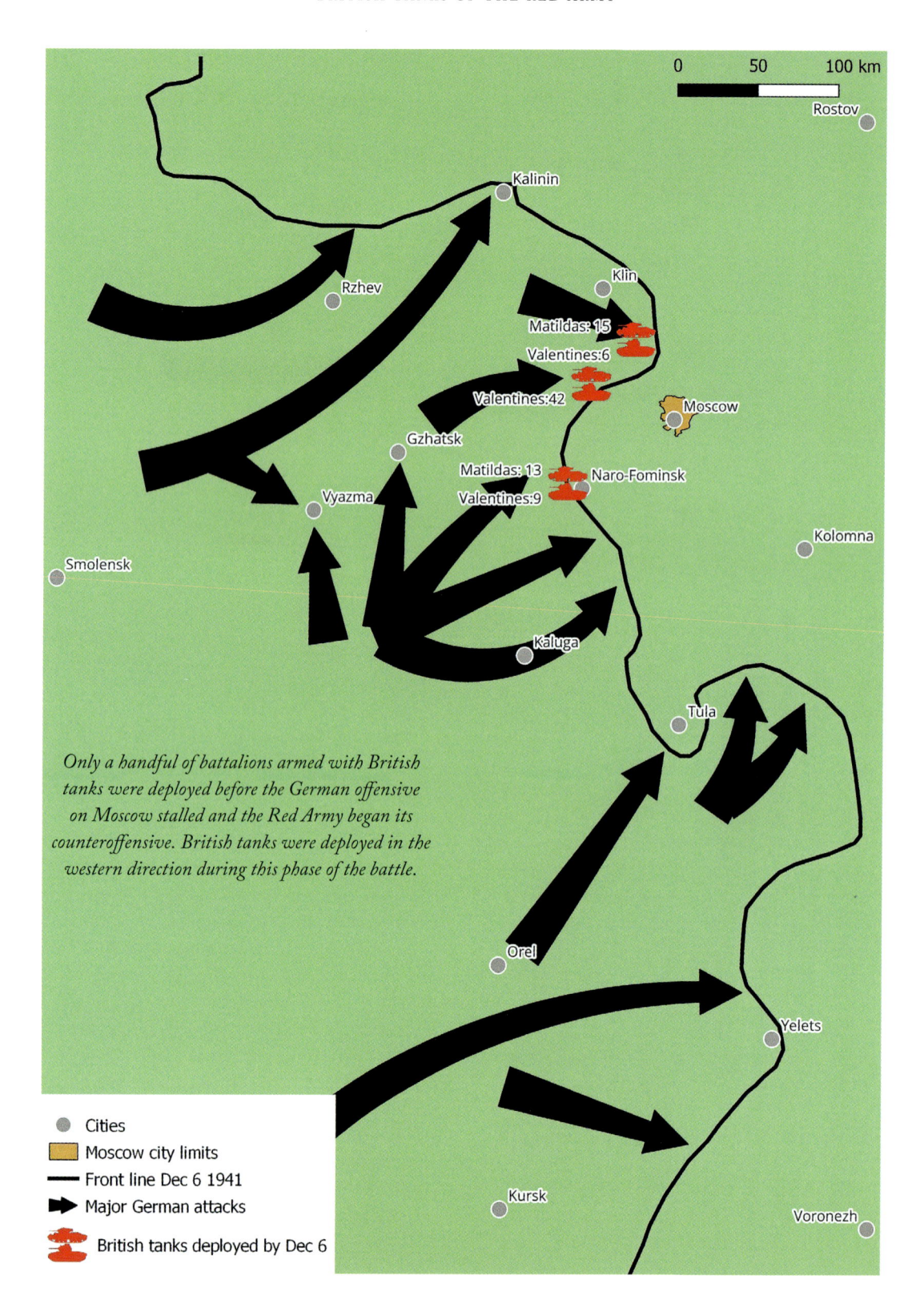

Only a handful of battalions armed with British tanks were deployed before the German offensive on Moscow stalled and the Red Army began its counteroffensive. British tanks were deployed in the western direction during this phase of the battle.

The 136th Independent Tank Battalion was the next Soviet unit to try out British tanks in combat. The battalion started out with an impressive force of 10 T-34s, 10 T-60s, nine Valentines, and three Matildas. The tankers began to study British tanks in Gorky on November 10 but as of December 1 their studies had to continue on the front lines.[250] On December 4, the battalion was attached to the 5th Independent Tank Brigade located in the vicinity of Tashirovo, north-west of Naro-Fominsk.

On the night of December 7, the brigade was ordered to destroy an enemy force that had broken through in the sector of the 222nd Rifle Division. The mission was completed successfully and the brigade returned to its initial positions.[251] The front remained static, but the 136th ITB continued to lose vehicles, presumably to breakdowns. The battalion had just four Valentines in service, plus nine T-34s and four T-60s by December 9. All Matildas and all but one Valentine ended up in repairs by December 15.[252] The battalion reported no permanent losses, and all of the knocked-out tanks were sent to be repaired.[253]

On December 15, the battalion was attached to the 329th Rifle Division and then rolled into the 20th Tank Brigade, with which it took part in the offensive phase of the Battle of Moscow.[254]

A month after the offensive began, the 136th ITB's commander composed a brief report on their experience with Valentine tanks: "Experience in using 'Valentine' tanks shows that: Mobility in winter is good. The tanks can move in soft snow 50-60cm deep. Traction on ground is good, but spurs are needed on ice.

"The gun works flawlessly, although there were cases of failure to return to battery after firing for the first five to six shots, presumably because the gun grease thickened. The guns are very sensitive to oiling and maintenance.

"Vision through slits and observation devices is good. The engine and transmission work well for 150-200 hours, after which a drop in engine power is observed. The quality of the armour is high ... Overall, the MK.III is a good fighting machine with powerful armament, good all-terrain mobility, capable of fighting enemy personnel, fortifications, and tanks.

"Negative aspects include: bad traction. The suspension bogeys are very vulnerable, if one wheel is destroyed the tank can no longer move. There are no HE shells for the gun."[255]

The 131st Independent Tank Battalion also received British tanks in 1941. As of December 5, it had five KV-1 tanks and 18 Valentines on hand. It was attached to the 112th Tank Division on December 18, at which point it had only one KV and "eight English tanks" left.[256] The division fought near Dubna (Tula oblast) at the time.[257] Unfortunately, surviving documents of the battalion and the division do not contain any detailed reflections on the performance of the Valentines in combat.

The 170th and 171st Independent Tank Battalions were formed in mid-December. The 171st ITB contained 12 Matildas (six with radios), nine Valentines (all with radios) and 10 T-60s. The vehicles were grouped into companies by type: the 1st company had Matildas, the 2nd had Valentines, the 3rd had T-60s. Training left much to be desired: the Matilda crews only had 10 days of training with their tanks and the Valentine crews were seeing these tanks for the first time.[258]

The 170th and 171st battalions were attached to the North-Western Front on December 20, where they were attached to the 27th Army (soon thereafter renamed to 4th Shock Army)[259] near Ostashkov. Even before the battle began, the 170th ITB reported that only seven Matildas,

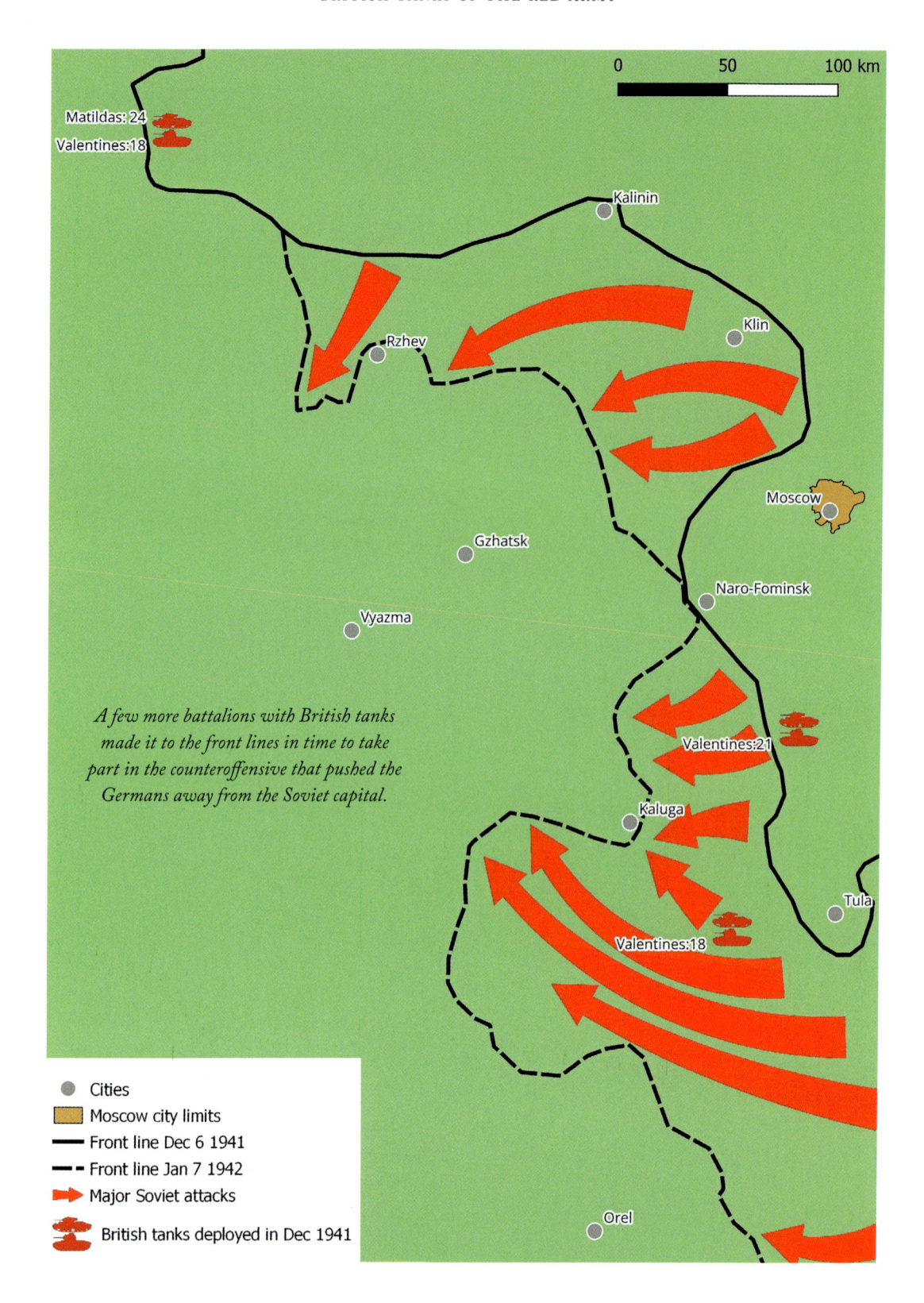

BRITISH TANKS OF THE RED ARMY

Matildas: 24
Valentines: 18

Kalinin

Rzhev

Klin

Moscow

Gzhatsk

Naro-Fominsk

Vyazma

A few more battalions with British tanks made it to the front lines in time to take part in the counteroffensive that pushed the Germans away from the Soviet capital.

Valentines: 21

Kaluga

Tula

Valentines: 18

Orel

- ● Cities
- ▇ Moscow city limits
- — Front line Dec 6 1941
- --- Front line Jan 7 1942
- ➤ Major Soviet attacks
- ♣ British tanks deployed in Dec 1941

72

nine Valentines, and 10 T-60s were in service. It's likely that inexperienced drivers were responsible for the five broken down Matildas.[260] The 4th Shock Army spent the rest of the year deploying for a counteroffensive and the British tanks did not see any combat in 1941.[261]

The 23rd Independent Tank Brigade was formed on December 12, 1941. On December 14, it was joined by the 132nd Independent Tank Battalion with "two companies of English tanks and a company of T-60s". The tanks went into battle in support of the 133rd Rifle Division of the 49th Army near Serpukhov on the next day. Here, the T-60 demonstrated perhaps its only advantage over the British tanks. The six-ton small tank could drive over ice, where the 16 ton Valentine or 25 ton Matilda could not.

As before, the brigade was pulled apart into individual companies by combined arms commanders, but brigade commander Ye. Ye. Belov still considered his tanks to have performed effectively. On January 2, 1942, he wrote to the commander of armoured forces of the 49th Army: "The English tank is a GOOD TANK when it comes to fire and manoeuvre, but it has a drawback: considerable sliding even on small slopes". By the commander's evaluation, the crews performed well despite their brief training period.[262]

Belov also praised the performance of British tanks in deep snow. All types of tanks in his employ worked well on paths packed by horse-drawn carts. The Matilda could drive in 3rd gear off-road in loose snow 40-45cm deep. The Valentine could navigate the same terrain in 1st and 2nd gear, which corresponded to a speed of 5-6kph. The T-60 could not drive in snow this deep without assistance. Belov recommended sending those tanks to flank through forests where the depth of snow banks was limited to 25-30cm. Without spurs, the Valentine and Matilda could barely climb 20-25° slopes, but the T-60's limit was 15-20°. The T-60 could descend down a 30-35° slope in zig-zags.[263]

Belov's assessment of the armament was not as high. The cannons had limited value when fighting infantry due to a lack of HE shells, and the machine guns jammed constantly. Belov also noted that his technicians had no repair manuals for their British tanks, which made using precious engine-hours to warm up the tank in the winter an expensive luxury.[264]

The contribution of British tanks to the defence of the Soviet capital is one of the most hotly debated topics in the history of British aid to the Red Army. While some claim that it was the arrival of British tanks that helped save Moscow in November 1941, it is hard to agree with this assessment.

Even though the first tanks arrived in the USSR in October 1941, it still took time to inspect them, prepare them for service, and train their crews. Matilda and Valentine tanks only began to reach the front line towards the end of the defensive phase of the Battle of Moscow when the German offensive had already run out of steam. Even then, these were not large tank units, but individual battalions and sometimes even companies armed with foreign tanks.

Only four battalions were deployed before the German offensive towards Moscow stalled and four more over the course of the next month. To put the numbers into perspective, a total of 13 tank brigades (39 battalions) and one tank division (nominally eight battalions) took part in the defensive phase of the Battle of Moscow.[265]

While it's hard to imagine that Moscow would fall without the timely arrival of British tanks, it is also incorrect to state that their presence was unwelcome. The Matilda and Valentine could hardly compete with the

KV-1 or T-34 in terms of armour, firepower, or mobility in deep snow, but one must also remember that Soviet tank production was at its lowest point in the war and the Red Army's losses in armour were at their highest. The armour and armament of British infantry tanks used in the Battle of Moscow still compared favourably to that of the T-60 and other light Soviet tanks, which were much more common.

Second Battle of Kharkov

After the Germans were pushed away from Moscow, the momentum of the Soviet counteroffensive began to slow and then petered out. The Eastern Front was no longer characterised by rapid and deep offensives, but by slow meat grinders reminiscent of the First World War. The spring mud season impeded the Red Army as much as it did the Wehrmacht. During this pause, the front line stretching from Leningrad to Rostov-on-Don bristled with trenches and fortifications.[266] This was an environment where slow moving but heavily armoured British tanks could excel.

One of the more advantageous launchpads for a new offensive established before the mud set in was a large bridgehead west of the Severskiy Donets river called the Barvenkovo Salient.[267] Here, the Red Army aimed to strike north at Kharkov, a city with a considerable industrial and political significance. If successful, this attack could set up a larger offensive all the way to the Dnieper. Given the scale of the counteroffensive carried out after the failure of Operation Typhoon in the winter of 1941, Marshal Timoshenko considered this goal to be achievable.[268] The Stavka was more sceptical, but nevertheless outfitted the South-Western Front with a large quantity of ammunition and reserves.[269]

As evacuated Soviet factories struggled to reach their former output beyond the Urals[270] and deliveries of foreign tanks picked up steam, the proportion of British vehicles on the front line grew. Out of 1,922 tanks that arrived in Red Army units in April 1942, 134 were Matildas and 144 Valentines. In May, the deliveries increased further to 255 Matildas and 171 Valentines out of a total of 2,723 tanks. While such high rates of delivery didn't last, they ensured that there were plenty of British tanks in the field by the summer of 1942.[271]

The composition of the 22nd Tank Corps of the South-Western Front reflected this variety. As of May 11, 1942, its 36th Tank Brigade had 10 Matildas (one in need of minor repairs), 20 Valentines (one in need of refurbishment), and 16 T-60s (two in need of minor repairs). The unit reported three loads of 76mm ammunition (suggesting that some of the Matildas were close support tanks armed with 3in howitzers), 3.8 loads of 40mm ammunition for 2-pounder guns, and three loads of British machine gun rounds.

The T-60s had three loads of 20mm shells and 1.5 loads of Soviet machine gun rounds. The 13th Tank Brigade had 20 Matildas (two undergoing repairs), 17 BT tanks, and nine T-26es. It reported 2.6 loads of 2-pounder ammunition, but only two loads of British machine gun ammunition and 2.7 loads of Soviet 45mm shells. The final 133rd Tank Brigade in the corps was equipped with only Soviet tanks: 19 T-34s (two in need of repairs), 13 BT-7s, and 8 BT-5s.

The brigade had two loads of Soviet 76mm rounds, 1.7 loads of 45mm rounds, and 4.3 loads of machine gun ammunition. In general, the British tanks of the 22nd Tank Corps had as much if not more ammunition available to them as the Soviet ones, showing that the conversion to use domestic weapons tested in late 1941 was no longer necessary. The status report also mentioned that the tank crews were poorly prepared, especially when it came to drivers in British tanks.[272]

The offensive began on May 12, 1942.[273] The 22nd TC went into battle on the first day, helping the 38th Army crack open the German defences. The 36th TBr was attached

26-Tonner m.J. Pz Kpfw **Mk II** (Matilda)

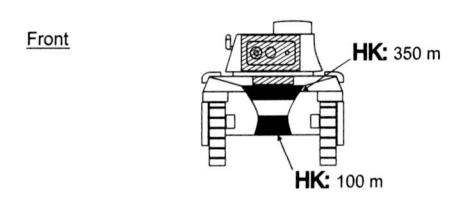

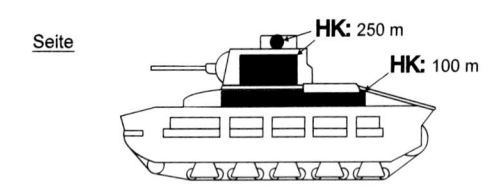

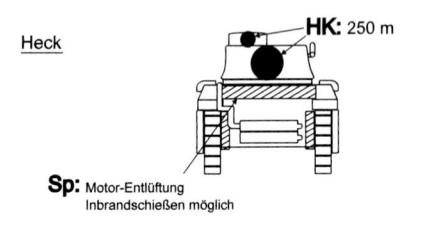

Front — HK: 350 m / HK: 100 m
Seite — HK: 250 m / HK: 100 m
Heck — HK: 250 m
Sp: Motor-Entlüftung Inbrandschießen möglich

A German instruction manual on engaging a Matilda tank with a 5cm KwK 40. Black areas indicate places where the main armour can be penetrated, hashed areas indicate places that can be hit to damage components without penetrating the tank's armour. Like the 3.7cm Pak, only tungsten carbide shot (HK) allowed for reliable penetration. From the rear, the engine could be set on fire with a high explosive shell (Sp) fired through the cooling system grilles on the engine deck.

26-Tonner m.J. Pz Kpfw **Mk II** (Matilda II)

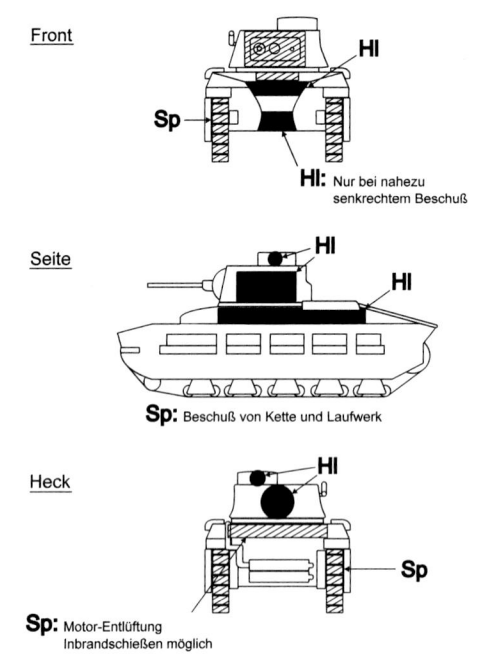

Front — HI / Sp / **HI:** Nur bei nahezu senkrechtem Beschuß
Seite — HI / HI / **Sp:** Beschuß von Kette und Laufwerk
Heck — HI / Sp
Sp: Motor-Entlüftung Inbrandschießen möglich

A German instruction manual on engaging a Matilda tank with a 7.5cm KwK L/24. The short 75mm gun could only hope to penetrate the Matilda's armour with HEAT shells or stop it by breaking the running gear with HE shells.

to the 226th Rifle Division in an attack towards Mikhailovka. The 133rd TBr was attached to the 124th Rifle Division to attack towards Peschanoye. The 13th TBr was kept in the second echelon where it would join two regiments of the 81st Rifle Division in an attack at Dragunovka.[274]

The attack started at 7.30am and progressed well. The 36th TBr routed its opposition at Nepokrytaya and pursued the retreating enemy towards Mikhailovka. Seven cannons and two warehouses were captured that day. The cost was light: 10 men were killed and 40 wounded. Two Matildas were knocked out and two more burned up. Six Valentines were knocked out and recovered. Two could be restored by the unit's workshops, but four more would have to be refurbished.[275] Six T-60 tanks were lost. Half could be repaired by the unit, the others would need repairs at a factory.[276]

Having taken Nepokrytaya, the brigade switched to a defence in anticipation of a German counterattack. The defence of Nepokrytaya lasted for five days. The 36th

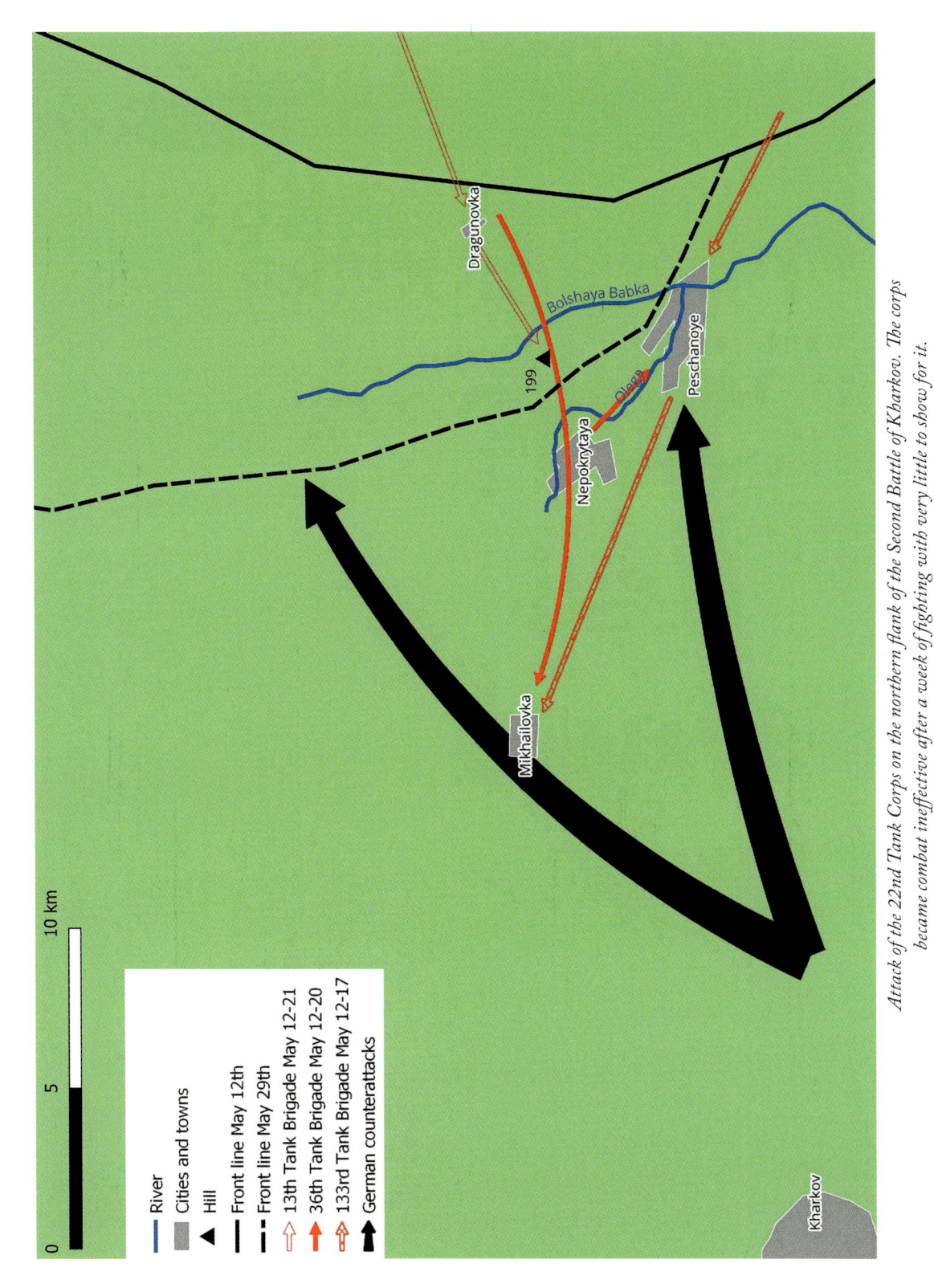

Attack of the 22nd Tank Corps on the northern flank of the Second Battle of Kharkov. The corps became combat ineffective after a week of fighting with very little to show for it.

TBr held, but at a heavy cost. Reinforcements that arrived on May 18 only filled up the brigade to 20 Matildas, 10 Valentines, and 16 T-60s. Along with new tanks, the 36th TBr had new objectives: attack Peschanoye in support of the 124th Rifle Division. Since the attack was to start immediately, there was no time to conduct reconnaissance or coordinate with the infantry. The brigade managed to enter Peschanoye, but could not hold it without infantry and was forced to retreat.

The situation repeated itself three times on May 19. To make matters worse, the bridgehead held by the 36th TBr south of the Olega river was very small and did not give a lot of room for the tanks to manoeuvre. As a result, losses from enemy artillery and aircraft were high. Out of 46 tanks, 26 were lost here, 16 of which were recovered. These losses were too great to continue. On May 20, the commander of the 38th Army ordered the brigade to withdraw.[277]

The 133rd TBr did not get far either. By May 13, the brigade settled down for a defence in Mikhailovka. Ten tanks were lost by May 14, five burned and five knocked out.[278] The brigade remained on the defensive until May 16.[279] This was also a costly process, and on May 17 the 133rd Tank Brigade handed over its remaining vehicles to the 36th TBr and relocated to Beliy Kolodez to receive new materiel.[280]

The 13th Tank Brigade followed in the second echelon and did not see battle on the first day of the offensive.[281] By the end of the day, the brigade crossed the river Olega and reached the Frunze farm. Like the 36th TBr, it settled here to defend against a large enemy tank counterattack.[282] Reports claim 30 enemy tanks destroyed on May 13 as well as an armoured car, an AA gun, six anti-tank guns, and eight machine guns. This victory came at a cost: 12 Matilda tanks, 16 BT tanks, and six T-26es were knocked out.

Fifty-six men were killed, 36 wounded, and 37 missing. Reinforcements were allocated on May 16 and the brigade went on the offensive once more.[283]

On May 18, the 13th Tank Brigade moved out to attack hill 199. Unlike the 36th Tank Brigade, the 13th TBr managed to establish proper cooperation with infantry of the 226th Rifle Division, but this didn't help.[284] Pressure from enemy anti-tank artillery forced the brigade to retreat, leaving its positions to infantry. Two Matilda tanks, six BTs, six T-26es and one T-34 were lost on May 18 and 19. Ten men were killed, including the commander of the 1st battalion Captain Dyukov, commissar of the 1st battalion Politruk Alekseev, and the commander of the 2nd battalion Major Krivoshey. 150 were wounded, including the commissar of the 2nd battalion Politruk Samoilov. 46 more went missing. These losses were unsustainable, and the brigade was pulled out on May 21 on the orders of the corps commander.[285] Just over a week into the offensive, the 22nd Tank Corps was rendered combat ineffective and pulled out to refit.[286]

The corps commander Major General Shamshin soberly analysed the reason for this failure. A considerable percentage of the losses were taken due to the way the corps was used in battle. Rather than striking as one, it was picked apart into its composite brigades, which were then individually assigned to support infantry divisions. In addition, the commander of the 38th Army bypassed the 22nd TC headquarters entirely and gave orders to individual tank brigades. In the meantime, the infantry the tanks were attached to knew little about how tanks operated and what support they needed. In his report, Shamshin stated the need to have a permanent brigade of motorised infantry attached to a tank corps, which would be much better trained to operate alongside tanks. Organic artillery was also needed, especially anti-tank artillery.[287]

The blame was not only placed on the infantry. The commanders of the 13th and 133rd Tank Brigades were chastised for inaction during battle.[288] Brigade commanders, staffs, and department chiefs stayed a considerable distance away from the fighting, unable to effectively command their vehicles or provide proper support.[289] Evacuation of damaged vehicles was also carried out poorly. Even though evacuation assets were available, the commander of the 36th TBr left 19 damaged tanks on the battlefield.

The tanks still had functional weapons and remaining ammunition, but they were abandoned by their crews and no infantry was assigned to guard them.[290] Communications were organised poorly and additional training for signals chiefs and radio operators was ordered at the end of May.[291] No specific complaints were made about the performance of the British tanks, despite the earlier remark about their insufficiently prepared drivers.

Battle of Voronezh

While the Battle of Stalingrad was no doubt the most famous German offensive carried out in the summer of 1942, German forces advanced on other parts of the front as well. One of these offensives was carried out east of Kursk, aiming to cross the Don and take Voronezh. The 11th Tank Corps of the 5th Tank Army was among the units taking part in this battle.

The 11th Tank Corps was formed on June 1, 1942. It consisted of the 53rd, 59th, 160th Tank Brigades as well as the 12th Motorized Rifle Brigade. The brigade's commanders were trained in Gorky, where the receiving centre for foreign vehicles was set up.[292] By July 4, elements of the corps were gathered north-east of Voronezh. Tanks were delivered to Dolgorukovo (some 100km north-east of Voronezh) by rail.[293] A significant force gathered here: 24 KV tanks in the 53rd TBr (two undergoing repairs), 88 Matildas split between the 59th and 160th TBr (six undergoing repairs), and 68 T-60s between the three brigades (one undergoing repairs). Ammo for the T-60s was scarce with only one load of ammunition available, but two to three loads of all other types were on hand as well as two to four loads of diesel and gasoline.[294]

The 5th TA ordered the 11th TC to move out on July 6. This was a difficult task, as heavy rains turned roads to mud.[295] While the KV-1 with its wide tracks could perform well in these conditions, the Matildas could not. For instance, the 160th Tank Brigade noted that only two of its Matildas managed to navigate a 400-500m long patch of mud, with the rest getting stuck.[296] Heavy bombing didn't help, but the corps only reported losses among its soft vehicles on that day.[297]

It didn't take long to encounter the enemy. Reconnaissance showed that the Germans were digging in just 50km to the south at Dolgoye and Zemlyansk.[298] Rather than attacking head on, the 11th Tank Corps was ordered to hit their western flank at Novosilskoye.[299] The delays during unloading and travel had an adverse effect on the execution of this attack. Only the 59th TBr and one battalion of the 12th Motorized Rifle Brigade made it into battle that day. With such meagre forces, the 11th TC was unable to cross the Kobylya Snova river that lay on the way to their objective.[300] Since the bridges were demolished, the night was spent erecting a temporary bridge. This work was completed by dawn.[301] Losses taken on July 7 were slight: one KV and one T-60 were damaged, one Matilda[302] (the corps reports two Matildas[303]) burned up.

The attack on July 8 was poorly coordinated. The 12th Motorized Rifle Brigade attacked at 7.30am, taking Khruschevo and pushing further to Ivanovka and Golosnovka. Meanwhile, the tanks of the 59th TBr only finished crossing the river at noon. One battalion attempted to circumvent the crossing and lost 13 Matildas in a swamp west of Ivanovka. The 160th TBr left a battalion in Yakovlevo to act as the corps commander's reserve.[304] The 53rd TBr finished crossing by the end of the day with 14 KV tanks and all of its T-60s.[305] Ten KV tanks were left behind: three were never unloaded, two had battle damage, and five broke down.[306]

The tanks that crossed encountered heavy resistance in the face of enemy anti-tank guns and aircraft. The offensive stalled, and an order was given at the end of the day to bypass the discovered strongholds.[307] This was a difficult day for the 11th TC, with a

26-Tonner m.J. Pz Kpfw **Mk II** (Matilda)

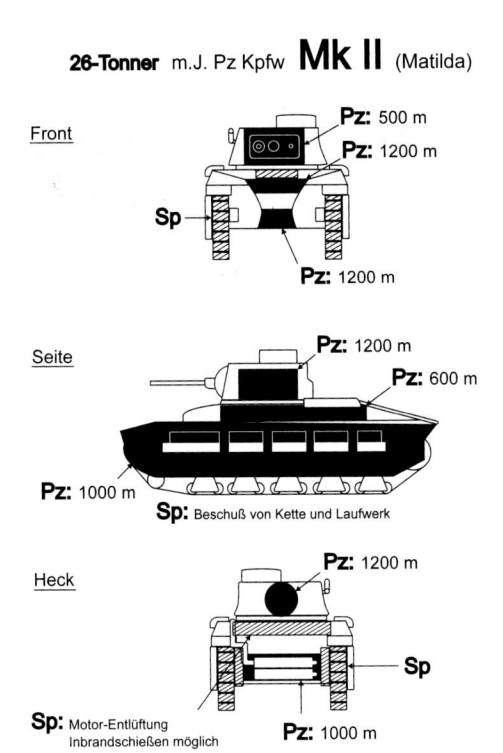

Front
Pz: 500 m
Pz: 1200 m
Sp
Pz: 1200 m

Seite
Pz: 1200 m
Pz: 600 m
Pz: 1000 m
Sp: Beschuß von Kette und Laufwerk

Heck
Pz: 1200 m
Sp
Sp: Motor-Entlüftung Inbrandschießen möglich
Pz: 1000 m

A German instruction manual on engaging a Matilda tank with a 7.5cm Pak 40 anti-tank gun. Black areas indicate places where the main armour can be penetrated, hashed areas indicate places that can be hit to damage components without penetrating the tank's armour. The new 75mm anti-tank gun could penetrate the Matilda's armour from a long range.

dozen Matildas lost in battle and two more broken down. Only three T-60s were lost in battle. The corps at this point was fairly thin on heavy and medium tanks. The 53rd TBr could bring 14 KVs to battle, but the 59th TBr was down to nine Matildas. The majority of medium tanks were in the 160th TBr with 20 in action and 20 in reserve. 90% of all T-60 tanks in the corps were still in action, 60 in total.[308]

The next day started with a German counterattack towards Ivanovka and Khruschevo. The counterattack was stopped, even though the 1st battalion of the 12th MRBr was routed. The offensive continued and by the end of the day the corps had reached the Sukhaya Vereyka river, although they were unable to cross it.

The offensive was impeded by heavy bombing, as well as a failure of the supply service to bring up fuel and evacuate damaged tanks in a timely manner.[309] On the next day the 11th Tank Corps engaged the enemy at Ilyinovka, where six to eight Matildas and two T-60s were lost. The tanks took their due from the enemy: 13-14 burned out German tanks and 20 cars were counted.[310]

The corps continued to take heavy losses, losing six Matildas and three KVs on July 11 from aircraft alone, as well as six heavy and medium tanks and six T-60s from enemy anti-tank guns. Just 13 heavy and medium and 20 small tanks remained by the end of the day. Exhausted, the 11th Tank Corps fortified in Spasskoye, defending against enemy counterattacks.[311] Even though the 11th TC was forced to retreat, all counterattacks were stopped at Kobylya Snova. Two more KVs and four Matildas were lost on July 12.[312]

Many awards were issued for these battles, including an Order of the Red Banner for Matilda gunner Sergeant I. Ya. Struts, who took part in five tank attacks in which he destroyed an enemy tank, three anti-tank guns, a car, and killed up to 50 Germans.[313]

This situation was common across the entire 5th TA, and by July 13 the entire formation was on a defensive footing[314] despite orders from the Bryansk Front to restore positions along Sukhaya Vereyka.[315]

The 11th TC had just 29 fighting vehicles left, although 13 were repaired over the next few days.[316] Even holding the line was not easy. A Matilda tank commanded by Lieutenant S. I. Zubarev took seven hits from enemy artillery, which jammed the driver's

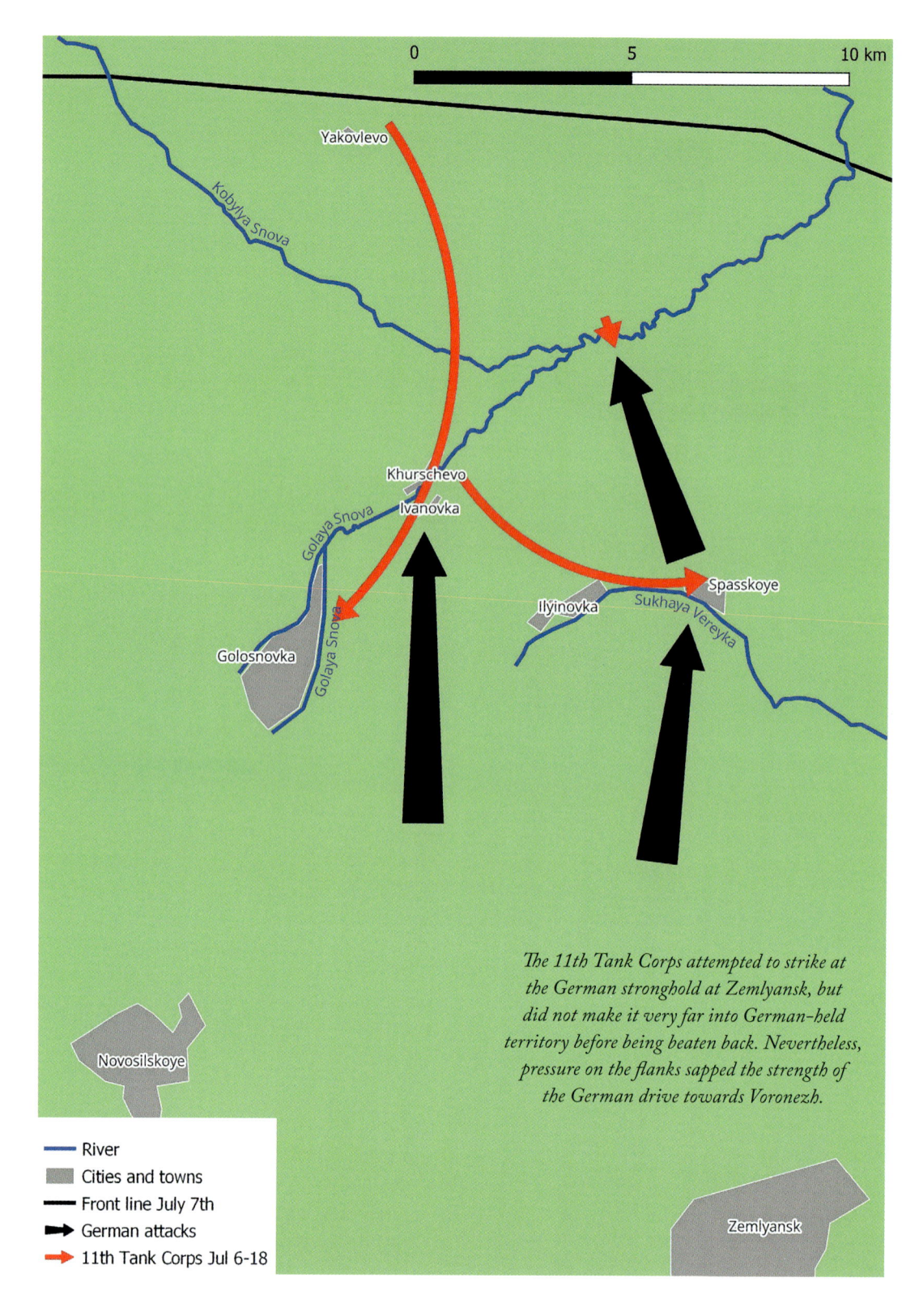

The 11th Tank Corps attempted to strike at the German stronghold at Zemlyansk, but did not make it very far into German-held territory before being beaten back. Nevertheless, pressure on the flanks sapped the strength of the German drive towards Voronezh.

hatch, destroyed the machine gun, and tore off the left side toolbox. Nevertheless, Zubarev repaired his tank and held his ground, earning him the Order of the Red Banner.[317]

Several more fruitless attempts to advance were made. The 5th TA was disbanded on July 18, with the 11th TC withdrawn into the reserve of the Bryansk Front.[318] The 11th TC was considerably battered, with the Matildas taking the most serious casualties. Out of 88 tanks initially available, 51 were lost irreparably with 22 more needing repairs. Out of 24 KVs, only eight were lost irreparably and nine needed repairs. The T-60s were in better condition with 17 lost irreparably and 30 needing repairs out of 68.[319]

This brief experience was enough to compile a report on how the Matilda performed. According to the Chief of Staff Colonel Kalinichenko, the engine was simple to service, but too weak for this tank. The compressor and pump for the hydraulic turret traverse broke often and were difficult to repair.

The transmission required constant care and took a very skilled driver to operate, otherwise various components wore out quickly. The tank's hull did not allow for easy access to components that had to be repaired often. The armour was thick but brittle and had many weak spots. The radio and intercom were easily damaged when the tank was hit, even if the shot didn't penetrate the armour.

Generally, the tank was considered to be very troublesome to maintain.

The turret jammed often, since there was no splash protection around the turret ring. The tracks also jammed when the skirt armour was hit, and even a small dent would immobilise the tank. The tracks generally were heavily criticised, as they were narrow and had poor traction, which had a negative impact on the tank's mobility. The tracks also tore easily and were difficult to repair.

The visibility from within the tanks was rated highly, except for the lack of vision devices for the loader. The sights were also considered modern. The 2-pounder gun was commended for its anti-tank performance, but the lack of HE shells was a drawback. The BESA machine gun was not rated as highly, as it jammed often. The rate of fire was limited by the poor ventilation system, as the fighting compartment filled up with fumes.

While accounting for the tank's drawbacks, the conclusions were generally positive.

"The MK-2 tank is a good means of fighting enemy tanks. It is reasonable to use them as stationary gun positions and best to use them on flat sandy or loamy terrain. When attacking enemy defences, it's best to use them in the second echelon following tanks with 76 or 75mm guns and use them as anti-tank weapons, as it is difficult for the MK-2 to combat enemy anti-tank guns. Drawbacks: poor manoeuvrability, speed, and off-road mobility."[320]

Battle of the Caucasus

A second supply route for foreign aid heading to the USSR was needed to avoid overloading the northern ports. Joint Anglo-Soviet occupation of Iran (Operation Countenance) in 1941 opened up a new route for British and American tanks, one that was safer than the Arctic convoys and faster than going through Vladivostok. Tanks arriving in Iran on British ships could either be delivered to Bandar Shah (modern day Bandar Torkaman) by rail and then to Baku by sea or driven to Tabriz on their own power. From there, they would be taken by rail to Stalingrad where the tanks would be forwarded to their units. Receiving departments were set up in Stalingrad, Baku, and Bandar Shah.[321]

The Germans weren't sitting still in the meantime. After the direct offensive on Moscow failed, their next blow was aimed at the south. The oil fields at Maikop, Grozny, and Baku could supply the Germans with the fuel needed to support a protracted war against the USSR. This was a tempting target, as Soviet reinforcements over the past year were focused on the north, particularly Moscow and Leningrad.

Tank units in the south were still equipped with obsolete pre-war light tanks, chiefly BT and T-26. As a result, deliveries heading through the south were redirected to equip local units for the upcoming fight with the Germans. NKO order #510 signed by Stalin on June 23, 1942, established several training units, in part those dedicated to training Soviet tankers to operate foreign tanks. Among them was the 191st Training Tank Brigade, founded from the existing 191st Tank Brigade.

The 191st had the unglamorous job of moving tanks during a leg of their overland journey, but as the situation on the North Caucasian Front heated up, the training brigade was dissolved to form three independent tank battalions: the 249th, 258th, and 563rd. The battalions were armed with the same tanks they were previously driving: the American Light Tank M3 and Canadian Valentine VII. Foreign tanks were also introduced into units returning from the front lines to refit.[322]

The 563rd ITB performed an interesting experiment before heading north to battle. Since the Valentines lacked any high explosive ammunition, an attempt was made to fire Soviet 50mm mortar shells from the British 2in bomb throwers. The results were quite effective. The shell could be fired at a range of 300-350m. The battalion reported their success to the commander of the Armoured Forces of the Northern Group of the Transcaucasian Front. The commander approved of this initiative, asking the Military Council of the Transcaucasian Front to issue 120 rounds of 50mm ammunition per Valentine tank: 1,080 for the 258th and 249th battalions and 1,920 for the 563rd.[323]

Time was of the essence. The Germans made significant progress towards the oil fields. Rostov-on-Don fell on July 24, and even though staunch resistance at Stalingrad pulled away some German forces, the rest were free to advance anywhere southwest of the Volga.

By the time fresh tank battalions were ready for battle, the German Army Group A was drawing close to the Main Caucasian Mountain Range. The commander of the North Caucasian Front, legendary Russian Civil War commander Marshal Semyon Budyonny, decided to draw a defensive line at the river Terek.[324] A small

16-Tonner J. Pz Kpfw **Mk III** (Valentine)

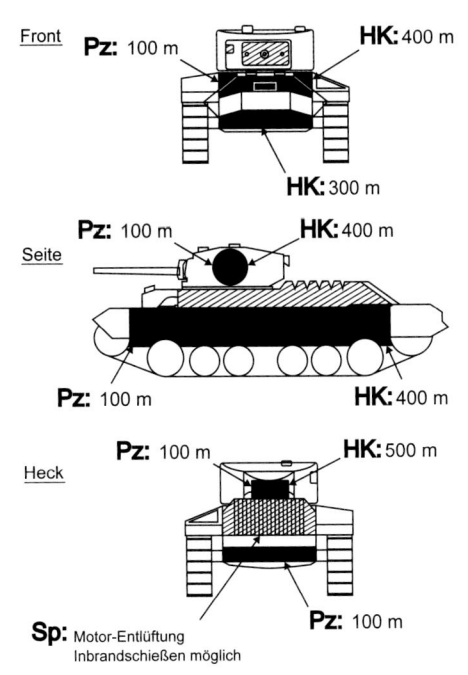

Front — Pz: 100 m, HK: 400 m, HK: 300 m
Seite — Pz: 100 m, HK: 400 m, Pz: 100 m, HK: 400 m
Heck — Pz: 100 m, HK: 500 m, Pz: 100 m
Sp: Motor-Entlüftung Inbrandschießen möglich

The Valentine was more vulnerable to the 5cm KwK 40 than the Matilda. Larger areas of its armour were vulnerable to tungsten carbide shot (HK) from a longer range and there were now openings for armour piercing (Pz) shells.

16-Tonner J. Pz Kpfw **Mk III** (Valentine)

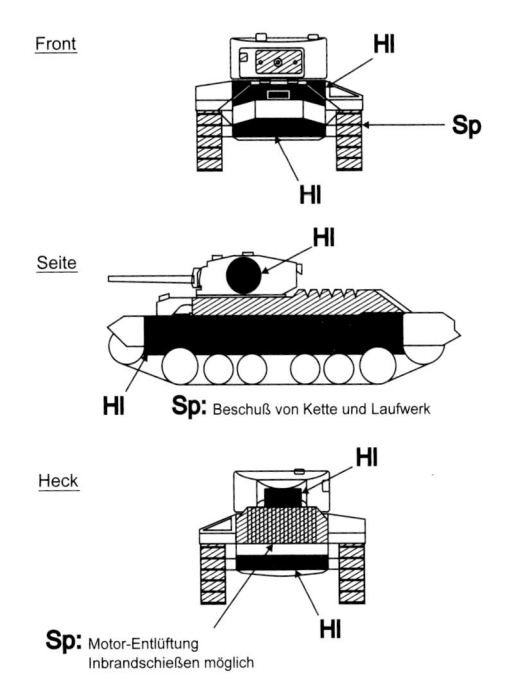

Front — HI, Sp, HI
Seite — HI, HI, Sp: Beschuß von Kette und Laufwerk
Heck — HI, HI
Sp: Motor-Entlüftung Inbrandschießen möglich

The situation when facing the 7.5cm KwK L/24 was the same. The main armour could only be penetrated with HEAT (Hl) ammunition. With high explosive shells, the gunner's only option was to disable the running gear or try to set the engine on fire with a shot from the rear.

town called Mozdok lay on the northern side of the river. To the south, the town of Malgobek stood in front of the vital Elkhotovskiye Vorota mountain pass that could have allowed the Germans to reach the Grozny oil fields. Valentine tanks made a considerable contribution to the defence of the North Caucasus as a part of the Mozdok-Malgobek Defensive Operation. 38 Valentines (chiefly Canadian) and 70 American M3 Lights arrived by August 24.

About 150 Valentine tanks would take part in the Battle of the Caucasus overall. This was a considerable proportion of the tank forces in the theatre. To put the numbers into context, the entire Southern Front that the Germans swept away on their way to the Caucasus had only one Valentine, one Matilda, 26 T-26 tanks, and 77 T-60s.[325] At the beginning of July 1942 the North Caucasian Front was similarly poor in tanks, with just three tank brigades and four independent tank battalions.

After receiving fresh reinforcements and absorbing 33 remaining tanks from the destroyed Southern Front,[326] this number grew to eight tank brigades and four independent tank battalions. Soon after, the North Caucasian Front was also

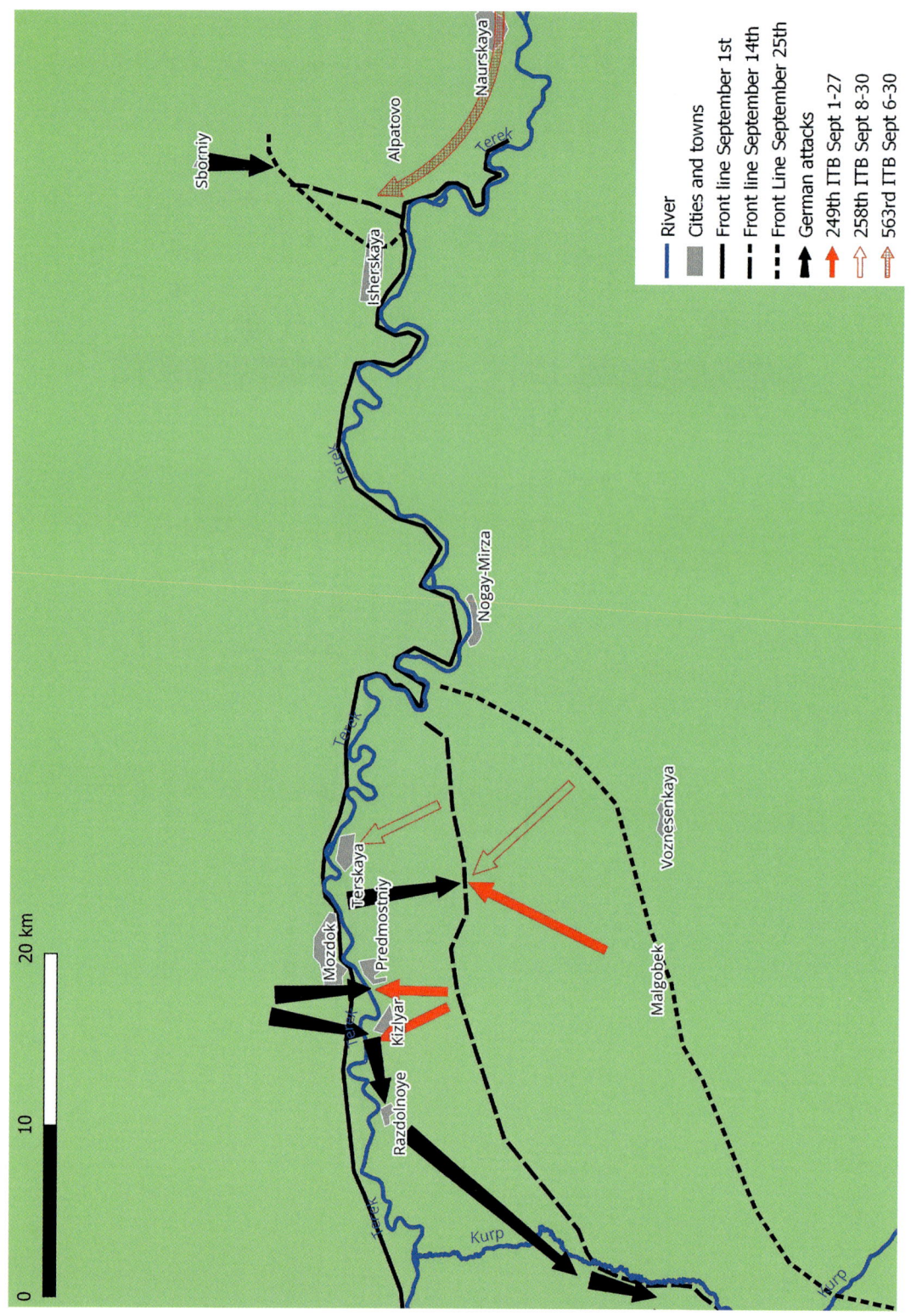

Valentine tanks made up a considerable portion of three battalions deployed to prevent the Germans from reaching the Elkhotovskiye Vorota mountain pass and crossing the Main Caucasian Mountain Range. Although all three battalions were pulled off the front line by the end of September, they did their part in protecting the Baku oil fields.

amalgamated, becoming the Northern Group of the Transcaucasian Front.[327]

The Soviet 9th Army was tasked with defending this critical passage through the mountains. Its forces were chiefly composed of infantry: the 151st, 389th, and 417th Rifle Divisions plus two brigades from the 11th Guards Rifle Corps attached as reinforcements. The 9th Army's attached 132nd Independent Tank Battalion consisted of 80 men with no tanks as of August 7.[328] The arrival of three tank battalions was quite welcome.

The 9th Army was opposed by General von Kleist's 1st Tank Army. Two of its divisions peeled off west, but the 9th Army was still facing down two tank corps and one army corps.[329]

Soviet historiography considers September 1, 1942 to be the start of the Mozdok-Malgobek Defensive Operation, but that does not mean that the front line was quiet until then. The situation at the end of August was already grim, with the 9th Army having lost control of the northern side of the river along with Mozdok and trying to repel German bridgeheads on the southern side.[330] The 249th ITB could not have arrived at a better time.

The 249th ITB went into battle at 3.30pm on September 2, 1942. Its objective was to support the 62nd Rifle Brigade near Predmostniy and Kizlyar, where several battalions from the 8th and 9th Guards Rifle Brigades of the 11th Gds RC were holding off a German landing force.[331] A force of 18 enemy tanks broke through the front lines and came within 7-8km of Predmostniy. A counterattack by a strike group consisting of the 62nd RBr and 249th ITB blunted the attack, destroying five enemy tanks.[332]

This success did little to push the Germans back across the river. There were not enough forces to contain the landing zone, and even though the 8th Gds RBr managed to successfully counterattack the Germans and knock them back out of Terskaya and the 9th Gds RBr was holding on at Kizlyar, German groups still penetrated the front line and were threatening to encircle the defenders.

Another wave of reinforcements was prepared: the 417th Rifle Division (less one regiment) and the aforementioned 258th Independent Tank Battalion. The 75th ITB (30 Light Tanks M3)[333] coming from Baku was also directed here. The commander of the 9th Army was ordered to use these reinforcements to clear the south bank of the Terek of all enemies.[334]

The situation at the front remained dire. The Germans attempted to expand their bridgehead yet again on September 5 and 6 with a force consisting of two infantry regiments and a large tank force. The 11th Guards Rifle Corps reported a force of 90 tanks,[335] the 9th Army's intelligence estimated 60 vehicles[336] and the Transcaucasian Front's reported a more reasonable 40-50.[337]

The one thing that the three levels of command agreed on was that the 62nd Rifle Brigade and the tanks from the 249th ITB were instrumental in stopping this attack.[338] The battalion itself reported that it knocked out 12 German tanks and 13 guns as well as capturing two Pz.Kpfw.III tanks at the cost of 14 tanks of its own knocked out and 10 burned. Five out of those 10 were destroyed by friendly fire.[339] By September 9, the battalion was on the defensive—protecting the road from Terskaya to Voznesenskaya[340] continuing occasional counterattacks.[341] On September 27 it was transferred to Karabulakskaya and put in the 9th Army's reserve.[342]

The 258th Independent Tank Battalion followed a similar path. It joined the fight on September 8, holding the enemy back at Terskaya. The battalion reported destroying 32 tanks, 21 guns, and 400 Germans between September 8 and 11. Eleven of its tanks were destroyed and another 11 were knocked out, nine of which were subsequently evacuated. The 258th ITB then held back the enemy from reaching Voznesenskaya, much like the 249th.[343] Also similar to the 249th ITB, the 258th was pulled out of fighting on September 30 and handed over all of its remaining vehicles to the 75th ITB on October 3, 1942.[344]

The 563rd ITB also took part in the fighting at Mozdok. As of September 6, it remained in the reserve of the Northern Group of the Transcaucasian Front to be used in a future offensive.[345] It entered battle on September 11, approaching Mozdok north of the river Terek from the east with the 10th Guards Rifle Corps.[346] Like with the 249th ITB, the battalion's objectives gradually shifted from swiftly destroying the enemy group in Mozdok to merely containing it from expanding east.[347] The battalion returned to the reserve of the Northern Group on September 30.[348] By this point it had 10 M3 Light tanks and six Valentines remaining.[349]

The defensive battles in the North Caucasus were difficult, but reinforcements continued to arrive, including Valentines. As of October 4, the 52nd TBr fighting south of Mozdok had three KV-1s, two T-34s, 10 T-60s, nine M3 Lights, and 10 Valentine VIIs (including two Valentines received from the 249th ITB). Reinforcements arriving in late September and early October had a larger proportion of foreign tanks. The 5th Gds TBr that arrived on September 29 had one BT tank, three T-34s, and 38 Valentines.[350] The 15th TBr that arrived on October 3 was armed with: one KV-1, five M3 Mediums, 10 Valentines and 24 M3 Lights.[351]

The battalions armed with Valentine tanks performed well in this battle. The commander of the 258th Independent Tank Battalion Major Yu. N. Karev received an Order of the Red Star for his unit's performance. The battalion under his command destroyed 32 tanks, 21 guns, and up to 400 German troops.[352] The Chief of Staff of the 249th ITB Senior Lieutenant I. G. Klimenko earned an Order of the Red Star as his battalion destroyed 38 tanks.[353] Several award orders note that Valentine tanks could take heavy damage from several dozen hits and still return from battle.[354]

While the Mozdok-Malgobek operation was not successful at keeping either city out of German hands, it achieved its ultimate goal. Despite the Germans feeding in a considerable quantity of reserves against the Northern Group of the Transcaucasian Front, they were unable to cross the Elkhotovskiye Vorota mountain pass and capture Soviet oil fields to the south. The timely arrival of Valentine tanks no doubt played a role in helping to contain German bridgeheads.

Even though British tanks came in handy during the crucial battles of 1942, they were not without issues. In a review of the tank battles of 1942, the Chief of Staff of Armoured and Mechanised Forces of the Red Army, Colonel Zayev, wrote: "Practice of using English tanks in battle showed that they were used in combat successfully, but there are considerable shortcomings present in their design and their use that negatively impact the use of these tanks on the front lines.

"The biggest drawbacks include: The cooling system of the MK-2 and MK-3 tanks is located in a difficult to reach place. The pipelines from the engine to the radiator run along the floor of the tank. In winter conditions, the water in the pipelines freezes even while the engine is running. This makes heating the tank complicated and makes it almost impossible to fill the cooling system with water in low temperatures.

"The design of the tank is complex, which means that repairs take three to four times longer. The manoeuvrability of the tanks and their mobility is very limited, especially in winter, due to their weak engines, high ground pressure (0.7-1.0kg/cm²) and poor traction. The cruising range is 70-100km.

"The MK-2 tank's spaced armour makes it complicated to replace components and assemblies of the running gear. If the armour is dented even slightly due to a hit from a shell, the track jams and the tank is disabled.

"The tanks are armed with 40mm guns and equipped only with 40mm solid shot designed to be used against tanks. Without an HE or HE-fragmentation shell, the tanks cannot effectively fire their cannons at enemy personnel and strongholds.

"Practice of using English tanks in battle allows it to establish that: It is reasonable to use these tanks in infantry support units. In order to improve the unit's firepower, it should include domestic tanks (T-34 and T-70). It is most reasonable to use these tanks in the southern theatre of war year-round. In other sections of the front, it is difficult to use these tanks in winter."[355]

Battle of Kursk

Even though deliveries of new Matilda tanks ended in the spring of 1943, the Red Army wasn't about to write off vehicles already in service. Continuing shipments of Valentines allowed the Red Army to refill units already armed with British tanks and let them continue fighting well into 1943, taking part in such famous actions as the Battle of Kursk.

One of these units was the 201st Tank Brigade. The 201st was a veteran user of British tanks, formed in the spring of 1942 in Gorky, where it received 26 Matildas and 20 T-60s.[356] The brigade fought on the Bryansk Front that summer until its strength was depleted. After passing on its surviving materiel to other units (including 15 Matildas to the 11th Tank Corps mentioned in an earlier chapter), the brigade was withdrawn for refitting.

It returned to the Voronezh Front in May 1943, this time attached to the 7th Guards Army.[357] At this point, it had 11 Matilda tanks on hand (two under repair) and 23 Valentines.[358] By the end of June 1943, its forces had grown to 18 Matildas (two of which were undergoing repairs as of June 30), 31 Valentines, and three T-34s.[359]

The 201st TBr took up defensive positions alongside the 73rd Guards Rifle Division and 1669th Anti-tank Artillery Regiment some 30km south-east of Belgorod. The tankers were supported by the 1529th Heavy Self Propelled Gun Regiment, one of two regiments armed with brand new SU-152 SPGs to take part in the Battle of Kursk.[360]

The German attack that came on July 5, 1943, fell short of their lines. In the evening of July 5, the brigade was instructed to gather at the Gremyachiy homestead, defeat the enemy attacking from the direction of Maslova Pristan' and Krutoy Log, and push them back across the Severskiy Donets river with a counterattack.

The attack came as expected on July 6 at 2pm.[361] After a probing attack with just two infantry companies and nine tanks, the Germans made several unsuccessful attempts to penetrate the defences at Gremyachiy.[362] The defenders claimed five enemy tanks knocked out that day in total. The Germans were said to make several attempts at recovering the tanks during the night, but constant fire made this impossible. The brigade's losses were relatively slight: just one Valentine was disabled as a result of hitting a mine.[363]

Frequent attacks continued on the second day of fighting. Soviet tanks chiefly fired from prepared positions with individual companies moving forward to support rifle regiments in threatened sectors. By 12.30pm, the brigade received worrying news. The neighbouring 211th Guards Rifle Regiment's 2nd battalion took heavy losses and was forced to retreat, baring the tankers' flank.

Thanks to the timely repositioning of the defending tanks and SPGs, the German attack was stalled long enough to deploy the 3rd battalion in the 2nd battalion's former positions. The 201st TBr continued to hold its positions against German attacks. With limited means of fighting infantry, the brigade's records credit the attached anti-tank gunners (which would have also been equipped with 76mm ZIS-3 divisional guns) and the SU-152s of the 1529th SPG Regiment with spoiling enemy attacks.[364]

Officially authorised artillery was supplemented by a "German self-propelled gun on the T-4 chassis" and a Soviet SU-122 which were found on the battlefield, repaired, and put into service.[365]

16-Tonner J. Pz Kpfw **Mk III** (Valentine)

Front
Pz: 1500 m
Pz: 500 m
Sp
Pz: 1500 m

Seite
Pz: 1500 m
Pz: 1500 m Sp: Beschuß von Kette und Laufwerk

Heck
Sp: Motor-Entlüftung Inbrandschießen möglich
Pz: 1500 m
Pz: 1000 m
Sp
Pz: 1500 m

Like the Matilda, the Valentine was very vulnerable to the 7.5cm Pak 40. This high velocity 75mm anti-tank gun could penetrate its armour at a very long range, in addition to being able to destroy the running gear and set the engine on fire with high explosive shells.

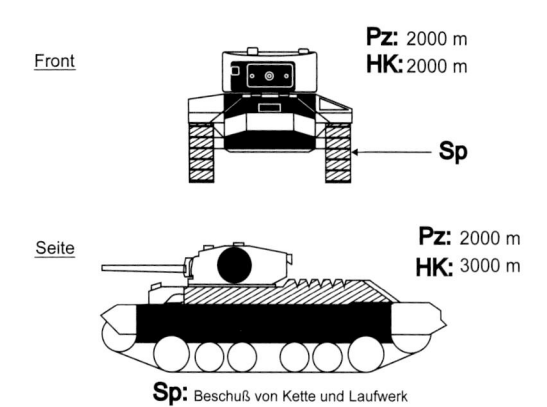

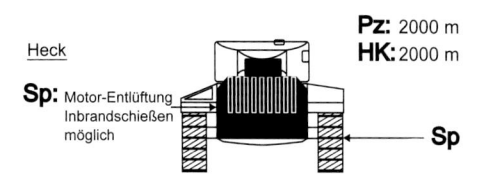

16-Tonner J. Pz Kpfw **Mk III** (Valentine)

Front
Pz: 2000 m
HK: 2000 m
Sp

Seite
Pz: 2000 m
HK: 3000 m
Sp: Beschuß von Kette und Laufwerk

Heck
Sp: Motor-Entlüftung Inbrandschießen möglich
Pz: 2000 m
HK: 2000 m
Sp

The Panther's 7.5cm KwK 42 was even more powerful than the 7.5cm Pak 40 and could defeat the Valentine's armour at very long ranges.

The brigade had a chance to conduct inventory on July 10. The fighting was fierce, with some crews taking part in as many as eight consecutive actions without a chance to rest.[366] Even so, the tanks were still in fairly good condition. One Matilda out of 18 was undergoing medium repairs.[367]

The Matilda's armour was still effective, as proven by Lieutenant S. I. Katalkin's tank. While on a reconnaissance mission, Katalkin came across a force of 10 German tanks. He only managed to knock out one enemy tank, but the rest were unable to penetrate the Matilda's armour and disengaged.[368]

The Valentines did not turn out to be as well armoured: out of 31 tanks, eight were total losses, five required medium repairs, and one was sent away on a mission. Two of the three T-34s were still in running order with one undergoing medium repairs. As one would expect from a relatively static defensive battle, plenty of fuel was available, but ammunition was running low with 1.25 loads left for tank guns and 1.2 loads left for small arms.[369]

The 201st TBr wasn't meant to stay in place forever. At 11pm on July 11, orders were given to support the 270th Rifle Division in a counterattack.[370] The redeployment of the 7th Guards Army was quick and a counterattack was launched at 10am on July 12.[371] This was largely successful, reaching the north-eastern outskirts of Krutoy Log, but it came at a considerable cost. The 201st TBr reported just six Matildas, 11 Valentines, and two T-34s operational on July 13.

Some of the losses were the fault of poor coordination between the 270th Rifle Division and the 296th Tank Battalion, which ended up going deep into enemy territory without any support. Unable to move up after them, the 201st TBr sent out reconnaissance groups to locate the missing tanks and crews.[372]

The 201st TBr once again switched to defensive positions. Limited support was offered to nearby infantry attacks.[373] While theoretically this allowed the brigade to restore some of its damaged vehicles, sending small packets of tanks to fight alongside unprepared infantry led to inevitable losses. The brigade was down to three Matildas and 12 Valentines by July 19. Both the SU-122 and captured German SPG were out of action.

Three new T-34s arrived as reinforcements.[374] Matilda tanks continued to display their tenacity; for instance, one sustained 69 hits in battle. The tank caught fire and the entire crew was killed or wounded with the exception of the driver, Senior Sergeant V. K. Yelizarov. He managed to put out the fire and recover the tank, receiving the prestigious Order of the Red Banner for his efforts, but such a heavily damaged tank could not be repaired on the front lines.[375]

The brigade soon resumed movement. On July 21, orders were given to move to a position 2km north-west of Pentsevo and prepare for another attack.[376] Preparations for the counterattack included a curious element. In addition to scouting terrain, reconnaissance groups were instructed to look for enemy tanks that could be repaired. One tank from both the 295th and 296th Tank Battalions was allocated to the recovery of captured tanks.[377] Either no suitable tanks were found or they could not be repaired in time as on July 24 the 201st Tank Brigade reported six Matildas, 13 Valentines, and seven T-34s in action.[378]

Concrete plans for an offensive were formed by July 27. The 201st TBr was attached to the 24th Guards Cavalry Corps and directed to attack west, towards Solomino and Tavrovo across the Severskiy Donets river. As Solomino was still held by considerable enemy forces, a plan was developed to flank them from the south by crossing at Toplinka.

The tanks neared the proposed crossing on the night of July 28-29 and concealed their tanks until the following night. The crossing was supposed to begin at 1am on July 30, but the engineering unit tasked with building a pontoon bridge across the river did a poor job, losing half of their pontoons in the process. The resulting crossing could not be used by tanks; the 201st TBr was recalled to initial positions at 2am.[379]

Without pontoons, the tanks would have to cross the old-fashioned way. A location suitable for fording was found and reinforced. A squad of five Valentines was the first to attempt a crossing. Four tanks crossed successfully, but the fifth got stuck in the mud. Attempts to pull it out with another Valentine proved unsuccessful; both the immobilised tank and the one sent to pull it out were knocked out by enemy artillery.[380] Four tanks that made it across were dug in to help the infantry defend their bridgehead.[381]

Moving tanks across the river was difficult, as the enemy was bombing the fording site constantly. One T-34 crossed on August 4[382] and six more tanks (three Valentines and three T-34s) on August 6.[383] These reinforcements came in handy, since the Germans tried to clear the bridgehead at 11.30am that day. Unfortunately, a counterattack ran into German SPGs in Toplinka, which resulted in the loss of four tanks.[384]

MATILDA AND VALENTINE TANKS IN COMBAT

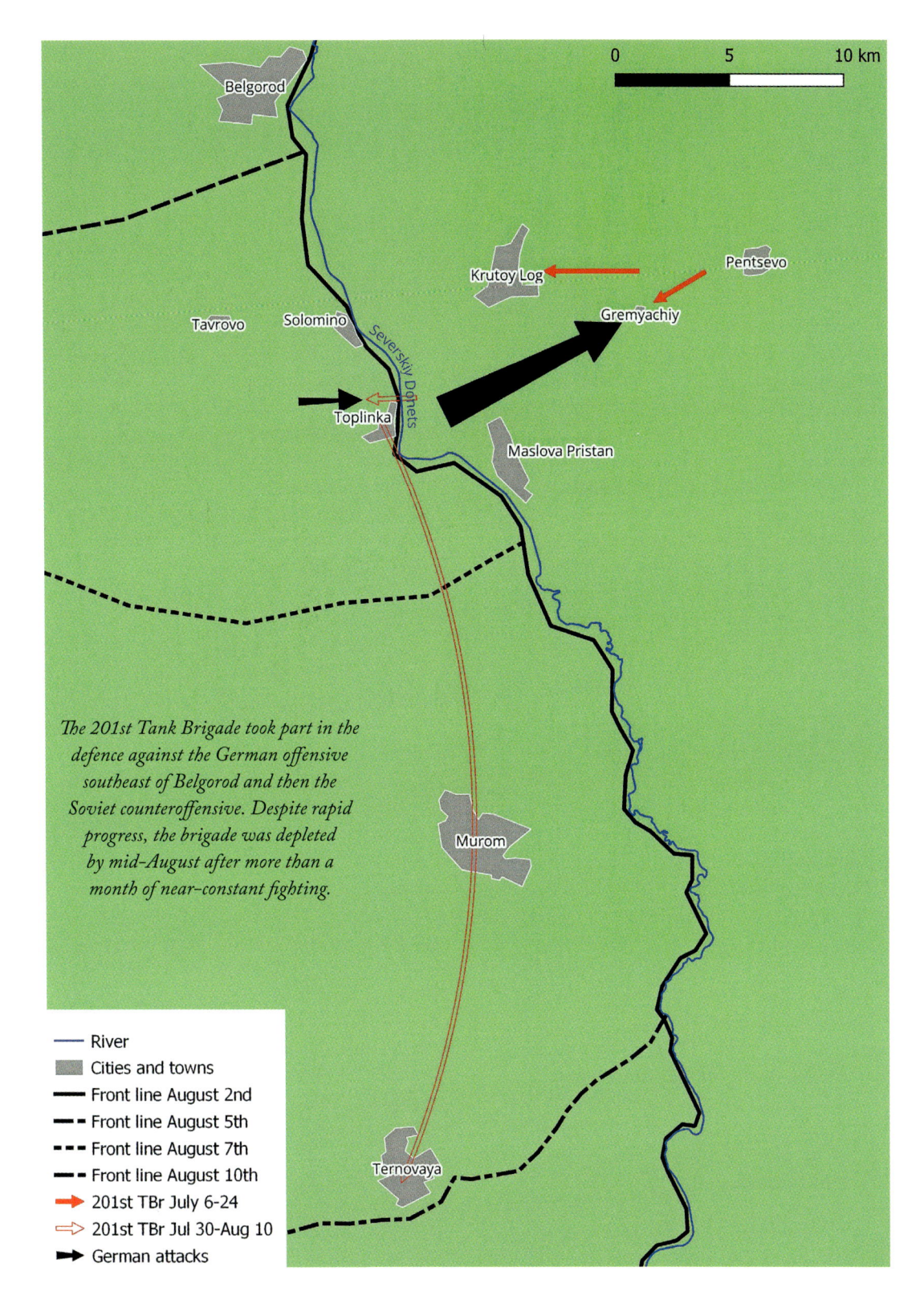

The 201st Tank Brigade took part in the defence against the German offensive southeast of Belgorod and then the Soviet counteroffensive. Despite rapid progress, the brigade was depleted by mid-August after more than a month of near-constant fighting.

- River
- Cities and towns
- Front line August 2nd
- Front line August 5th
- Front line August 7th
- Front line August 10th
- 201st TBr July 6-24
- 201st TBr Jul 30-Aug 10
- German attacks

As the situation across the entire Kursk salient became untenable for the Germans, they began to fall back. The enemy continued to bombard the crossing near Toplinka even as they retreated south. Nevertheless, the German resistance was not what it once was. The commander of the 201st TBr ordered the restoration of the river crossing and evacuation of all knocked out vehicles. Surviving tanks would pursue the enemy.

With just 14 tanks (five Matildas, five Valentines, and four T-34s)[385] and a company of motorised riflemen (infantry of the 78th Guards Rifle Division fell behind) the 201st TBr took Murom by 7.30am and then Ternovaya at 10am on August 9. A considerable number of trophies were taken with no losses in materiel.[386] Not every day of the offensive phase of the Battle of Kursk was this easy, but the brigade was able to maintain its numbers by repairing tanks.

Two T-34s, seven Valentines, and five Matildas were operational by August 10.[387] This was only a temporary solution and despite a stop to refit taken on August 15 the brigade had been ground down to the bone. Surviving tanks (one Matilda and two T-34s) were passed on to the 167th Tank Regiment.[388]

With extensive experience in using British tanks, the commanders of the 201st TBr were able to compose a detailed report.

Experience at the Battle of Kursk no doubt coloured the contents, as the report began by describing the tanks' inability to fight Panther, Tiger, and even Pz.Kpfw.IV tanks. The lack of an HE shell was also listed as a drawback. On the other hand, both the 2-pounder and the BESA machine gun were found to be very reliable.

Ammunition storage could be increased past the official amount: up to 110-120 rounds for the main gun could be carried and 18 ammunition belts could fit in each BESA ammunition box instead of 13. The 201st's report also mentions the ability to fire Soviet 50mm mortar shells out of the 2in bomb throwers, although this trick could result in the fins tearing off the shell and jamming the launcher. The 3in howitzer was received poorly due to its low muzzle velocity and range.

The engines of both the Valentine and Matilda were found to be reliable, although the compressor required a very careful touch. On the other hand, the transmissions were prone to fouling up with oil and slipping. Sharp turns could also result in broken-off gear teeth.

The running gear of the Matilda was criticised heavily, as the return rollers quickly jammed and tore at the tracks, resulting in loss of power. Grinding from the tracks would then ruin them completely after just 15-20km of driving.

The Valentine's running gear was much better received, although it was noted that the rubber tyres could fall off while driving. The idlers of the tanks were deemed weak as they broke off easily. The track links were also weak, particularly in winter, when they could shatter during driving. Both the Valentine and Matilda were found to require a full replacement of bearings in the running gear after just 400-500km of driving. The Valentine was considered to be easy to repair in the field (provided one could pick replacement parts off destroyed tanks, as spares were never available) but the Matilda was not.

In conclusion, the tankers state that in 1942 the Matilda and Valentine proved to be useful as infantry support tanks and could even fight German Pz.Kpfw.III and IV tanks at close range. However, by 1943, their armament was no longer sufficient. Mobility was judged as poor compared to the T-34 in all conditions. Off-road mobility in snow was also brought up.

The tank was found to be able to push through snow banks up to 60cm deep, matching the results achieved during official trials. The Valentine was considered to be a good tank with its only significant drawback being a weak gun without an HE shell.

The Matilda was found to be inferior to its fellow infantry tank in every respect. Even so, the report considered both tanks to be usable in secondary directions where encounters with enemy tanks were unlikely.[389]

Operation Bagration

As the war continued, Matilda tanks began to vanish from the Red Army's ranks. They were still occasionally seen in second rate units, but the tank's time in the spotlight was clearly over. This was not the case for the Valentine. Soviet tankers always preferred it to the Matilda, and the introduction of a 6-pounder gun gave the tank a new lease on life. These tanks remained in use throughout 1944 and 1945 even in the most vital operations.

One of these operations was the Belorussian Offensive Operation, better known under its codename Operation Bagration. This was a massive offensive carried out by four of the Red Army's Fronts aimed at liberating Belarus and destroying Army Group Centre. The high speed at which the offensive was scheduled to proceed required combat vehicles to play a major role, including tanks.

One of the most prominent users of Valentines in this operation was the 5th Guards Tank Army of the 3rd Belorussian Front with 38 Valentine IX tanks (referred to as MK-9) scattered throughout its composite units as of June 23, 1944. Three Valentines and three T-34s were used by the corps HQ. Two of the corps' brigades (3rd Guards and 18th Guards) were armed entirely with T-34s, but the 19th Guards Tank Brigade was equipped with 43 M4A2 Shermans, 25 Valentines, and one T-34.

The 10th Guards Motorcycle Battalion also had 10 Valentines and seven GMC T48 tank destroyers (called SU-57 by the Soviets). Artillery support was all of Soviet make, consisting of 18 ISU-152 SPGs from the 376th Heavy SPG Regiment, 19 SU-85 tank destroyers from the 1436th SPG Regiment, and 22 SU-76Ms from the 1496th SPG Regiment.[390]

The 19th Gds TBr reported just receiving its foreign tanks on June 12, 1944, making it unlikely that the tankers would have had much time to get acquainted with their new vehicles.[391] One of the causes was the secrecy surrounding the operation. Even though the tanks were kept a one- to two-day march away from the front lines, trains with new materiel came only at night and vehicles moved without the use of headlights.

Only staff cars with proper passes were permitted to move during the day. The tanks were camouflaged and waited their turn.[392] In the meantime, as much work as possible was done on paper. Neighbouring units coordinated their actions, with commanders personally inspecting the routes their units were going to take.

Crews were given instructions on operation of tanks in the forested swamps that made up the majority of terrain they were going to encounter in this operation. Tanks were also equipped with two or three logs to get through particularly muddy regions or build bridges across small water obstacles. Twenty metres worth of engineering bridge sections were allocated to each tank brigade. Finally, each tank corps was issued five military tractors in addition to three armoured prime movers for each of their brigades. All mobile workshops were restocked. The tanks had everything they needed to keep moving in any conditions.[393]

The 5th Gds TA was tasked with exploiting the breakthrough made by either the 11th Guards Army or the 5th Army. Depending on the conditions created during the breakthrough, the tankers had several routes to follow, all of which ended with reaching the Moscow-Minsk highway and seizing Barysaw. Once there, its mission was

MATILDA AND VALENTINE TANKS IN COMBAT

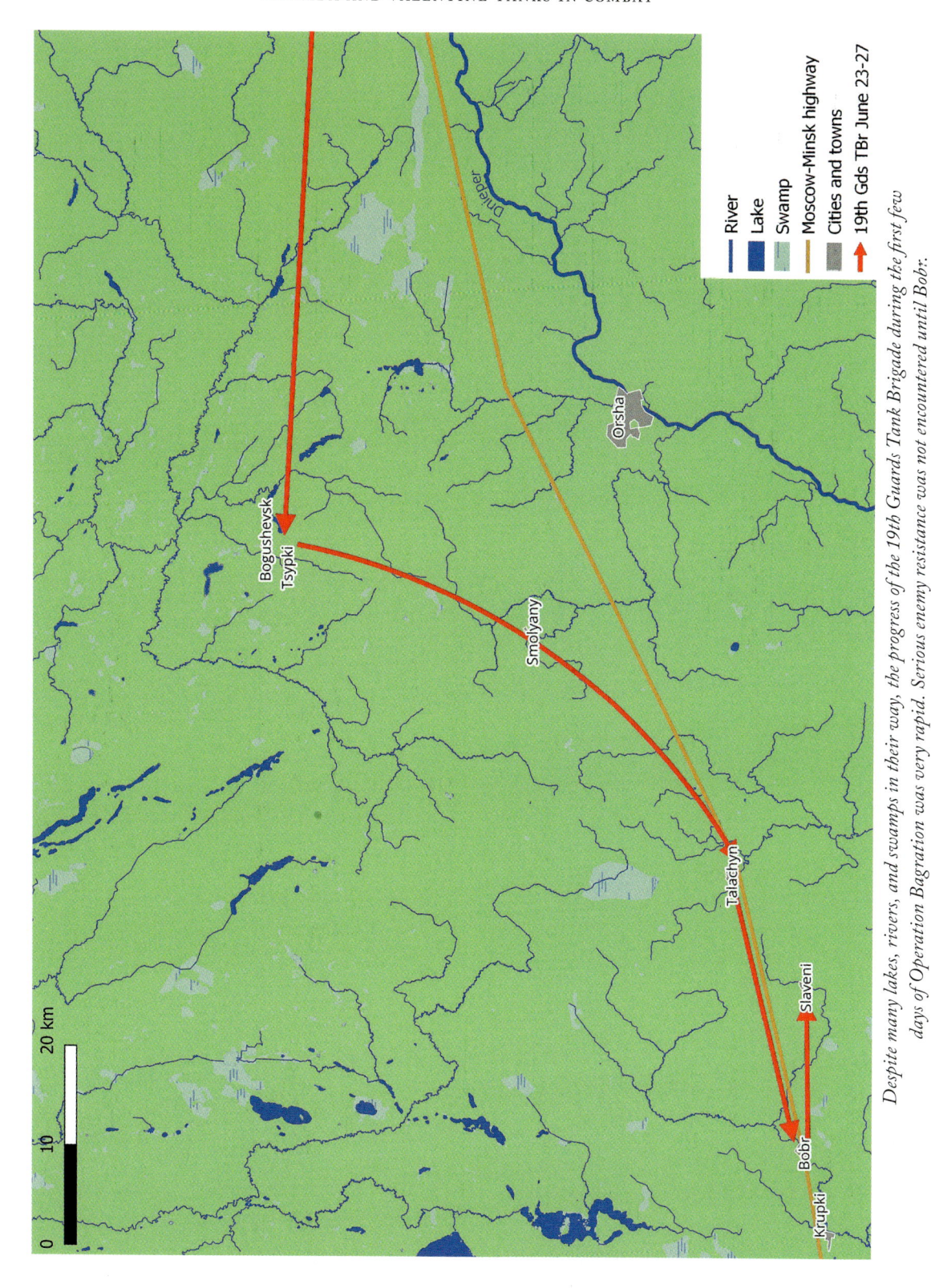

Despite many lakes, rivers, and swamps in their way, the progress of the 19th Guards Tank Brigade during the first few days of Operation Bagration was very rapid. Serious enemy resistance was not encountered until Bobr.

to create a bridgehead across the Berezina river that would be used as a staging ground for the 3rd Belorussian Front's attack on Minsk.[394]

The enemy's defences were softened enough by June 23 to predict where the breakthrough was going to happen. The 5th Gds TA was in position by 7am on June 25. The 3rd Guards Tank Corps that the 19th Gds TBr belonged to formed up on the Army's left flank at Svetitsy, Paruli, and Losevo.[395] The 19th Gds TBr was included in the Corps' vanguard.[396]

The plan was to wait for nightfall, but due to favourable conditions on the front line the order to attack was given earlier. The vanguards of each of the 5th Gds TA's tank corps moved out at 10am[397] and the rest of the army was in motion by 2pm. The vanguard of the 3rd Gds TC was in Tsipki by 9pm, having completed a march of some 90km. No enemy resistance was encountered.[398] Three Valentines fell behind due to technical faults.[399]

After a brief rest, the corps resumed movement at 1.20am on June 26, turning south towards Smolyany.[400] The vanguard encountered a small enemy rear guard there at 5am, but this did not prove to be a serious obstacle. Continuing onwards, the brigade took Talachyn by 6pm.[401] Reaching the Moscow-Minsk highway was a considerable achievement, as this blocked a quick retreat for the Germans left defending Orsha, putting them in a precarious position.[402] This position could be exploited by someone else though, as the 5th Gds TA was still pushing towards its main target: Barysaw.

Taking Talachyn was a significant achievement for the 19th Guards Tank Brigade, as evidenced by the number of awards issued for this occasion. Valentine crews got their share of decorations. Guards Lieutenant I. A. Pasechnikov, commander of a Valentine platoon, received the Order of the Patriotic War 1st Class for being the first to enter Talachyn and disabling a locomotive, allowing the capture of a train with supplies.[403]

Another platoon commander, Guards Lieutenant A. D. Pakharukov, received the same order for destroying a number of high-profile targets, including a Panther tank.[404] Valentine tank driver Guards Sergeant M. D. Klochkov received the Order of the Patriotic War 2nd Class for crushing an artillery battery under the tracks of his tank.[405] This is only a small portion of commanders and crewmen of Valentine tanks were distinguished in this battle.

Having reached the highway, further movement west was a lot simpler,[406] but not for long. The vanguard of the 3rd Guards Tank Corps encountered fierce enemy resistance at Bobr in the afternoon of June 27.[407]

While the main forces of the corps took the settlement by 3pm, the 19th Gds TBr retreated to Slaveni in order to rest.[408] The brigade was subsequently withdrawn into the corps commander's reserve.[409] It was not destined to idle for long, as the main body of the corps continued onward, reaching Krupki by 8.15pm on June 28. Progress was slowed by not only pre-arranged rear guards, but also retreating enemy forces trying to break through to the last strongholds of German resistance.[410]

The 19th Gds TBr was still not taking part in the main offensive, but deployed to blunt enemy counterattacks. By July 29, the unit was in poor shape with 19 Shermans, 16 Valentines and one T-34 remaining—or about half of the tanks it started out with.[411]

Having reached the river Berezina, it was clear that the Germans weren't going to make the crossing easy. The river was lined with pillboxes, earthworks, and other

MATILDA AND VALENTINE TANKS IN COMBAT

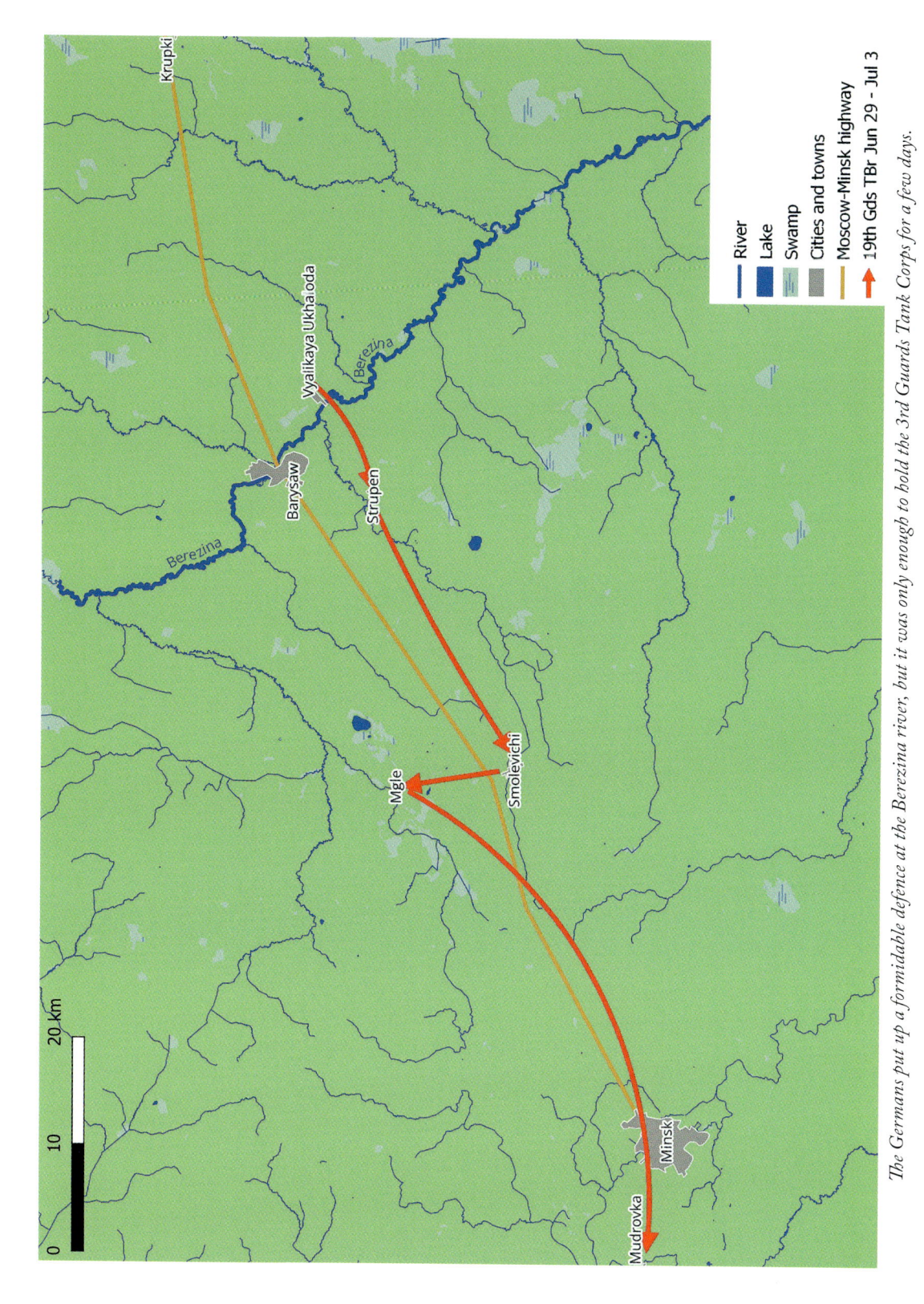

The Germans put up a formidable defence at the Berezina river, but it was only enough to hold the 3rd Guards Tank Corps for a few days.

defensive fortifications. Reconnaissance also spotted five Tiger tanks actively firing at the approaching units.[412] These were Tigers from the German s.Pz.Abt.505, which were also at Bobr a few days earlier.[413] Since there was no point in sending the battered brigade face-first into a Tiger ambush, the 19th Gds TBr was sent on a roundabout journey to Vyalikaya Ukhaloda in order to strike at Barysaw from the south with the help of the 18th Gds TBr.[414]

They crossed successfully, aiming to consolidate their forces in Strupen. This was achieved by 8.30pm on July 1, but at a considerable cost. The brigade lost nine Shermans burned up, four Valentines burned up, and three more damaged.[415] As the 18th Gds TBr was also badly hurt, it did not take part in the fighting that day.[416]

Unbeknownst to them, the Tigers left as the German defences began to crumble.[417] Elements of the 3rd Gds TC began their crossing on the night of July 1 and the city was liberated on the same day. The 19th Gds TBr continued its rapid advance westward, turning north at Smolevichi and reaching Mgle on July 2. The brigade was once again withdrawn into the corps reserve[418] as it was down to only 15 functional tanks.[419]

The Valentines ended this stage of the battle on a high note. A company of them led by Guards Lieutanant P. N. Nikiforov skilfully attacked the railway station, destroying four artillery batteries with no losses. Continuing the attack, Nikiforov's unit prevented a large enemy force from escaping to Minsk at the cost of just two tanks. These actions earned him the Order of Alexander Nevsky.[420]

The Berezina was the last large obstacle for the 3rd Gds TC. The tankers kept moving forward quickly, liberating Minsk by the end of the next day. The 19th Gds TBr ended the day in Mudrovka, just west of Minsk.[421]

Here, the brigade took a pause to rest once again.[422] The second stage of Operation Bagration was over.[423]

The 5th Gds TA tallied up its losses. The fast-paced campaign was a costly one. Out of 38 Valentine tanks in service with the 3rd Gds TC at the beginning of the operation, 29 were lost. However, only nine of those losses or 31% were total write-offs. The Valentine turned out to be much more tenacious than the Sherman (25 out of 35 knocked out tanks were irreparable or 71%) and even the T-34 (59 out of 97 or 61%).[424]

The report concludes with a commendation of the 5th Gds TA's units for covering a considerable distance across difficult terrain in a short time with an average pace of 60km per day. Almost always in the vanguard of the 3rd Gds TC, the Valentines showed that their often-derided speed was quite enough to support a lengthy and rapid thrust.[425] For its performance in the operation, the 19th Gds TBr was awarded the Order of the Red Banner and the battle honour of Minsk.[426]

Despite this performance, Operation Bagration was the Valentine's swan song. As the war continued, tank brigades traded in their foreign tanks for domestic ones. The aforementioned 19th Gds TBr had lost all of its Valentines by the end of July.[427] Only T-34-85 tanks were received as reinforcements on August 2.[428] With no replacements coming, just one Valentine was left in the entire 3rd Gds TC by the end of August 1944.[429]

However, the Red Army did not consider the Valentine obsolete even in 1945.[430] Small numbers of Valentine tanks were still issued to reconnaissance units. For example, at the start of the Vistula-Oder Offensive carried out in January-February 1945 the 57th Motorcycle Battalion attached to the 1st Mechanised Corps of the 2nd Guards Tank Army had 10 Valentine IX tanks.[431]

The 17th Guards Motorcycle Battalion attached to the 9th Gds TC of the same army also had 10 Valentines.[432] Valentine tanks remained in use with the Red Army until the very end of the Second World War. Forty were used by the 267th Tank Regiment attached to the 59th Cavalry Division, which was a part of the joint Soviet-Mongolian Cavalry-Mechanized group commanded by Colonel General Issa Aleksandrovich Pliev in the Soviet-Japanese War of 1945.[433]

Valentine Bridgelayer, Patriot Park. These tanks were used by the Red Army until the very end of the Second World War. PAVEL BOROVIKOV

III.
British Light Tanks and Cruisers in the USSR

THE MAJORITY of publications dedicated to the use of British vehicles by the Soviet Union focus on infantry tanks: Matilda, Valentine, and Churchill. These tanks were found to be satisfactory by the Red Army and ordered in large numbers to fight on the front lines.

However, not all types of tanks sent by Great Britain were so lucky. The story of British tanks in the Red Army would not be complete without a mention of the tanks that were sent to the USSR, tested, and ultimately rejected.

Light Tank Mk.VII (Tetrarch)

The Red Army knew very little about British tanks before the start of the Great Patriotic War, and this included light tanks. The first accurate information about these vehicles was obtained as a part of negotiations for purchasing British aid in the fall of 1941. The data obtained described the Light Tank Mk.VIB, Light Tank Mk.VII, Cruiser Tank Mk.I, Mk.II, and Mk.IV.[434]

The Light Tank Mk.VIB was a product of the British pre-war light tank concept and the most numerous member of the Light Tank Mk.VI family. Its armament consisted of just two machine guns, a .50in and a .30in. The 14mm thick armour protected only against rifle fire.

The tank's main weapon and method of protection was its top speed of 56kph, which could theoretically allow it to leave an unfavourable engagement.[435] In practice, these tanks performed poorly in France and the British themselves considered them obsolete as a fighting vehicle.[436]

The Light Tank Mk.VII or Tetrarch[437]

Tetrarch tank, Patriot Park. This is one of the 20 Tetrarchs sent to the USSR. The tank was found to be unsatisfactory and no deliveries were made after the first batch. PAVEL BOROVIKOV

The same tank from the other side. The complex running gear allowed the driver to make fine course corrections at high speeds by turning one of the road wheels and flexing the track. PAVEL BOROVIKOV

was a departure from the British light tank tradition. It was a grassroots development from Vickers-Armstrongs, although General Staff specification A17 was retroactively developed in 1938 for this tank. Unlike the Light Tank Mk.VI that was armed only with machine guns, this tank carried a 2-pounder 40mm cannon. At 7.5 tons, it was considerably heavier than the five ton Light Tank Mk.VI, but the extra weight came with a more powerful engine. The 165hp Meadows MAT gave the Tetrarch a top speed of 64kph.

A complex turning mechanism allowed it to turn its wheels and flex its tracks slightly to turn without losing speed. This method had a very wide turning radius, so it could only be used for fine course corrections. Tighter turns could be made with more traditional skid steering.[438]

The Light Tank Mk.VII (mistakenly labelled Light Tank Mk.VIII in the memo) was described to the Soviets as a "fast reconnaissance vehicle, available in small numbers".[439] Indeed, production of the Tetrarch was temporarily stopped in the spring of 1941 due to damage to the Metropolitan-Cammell factory from German bombs.[440] The report also stated that 35 tanks were due before the end of the year, after which the Tetrarch would be replaced by a better armoured variant (Light Tank Mk.VIII or Harry Hopkins) in 1942.[441]

The lightly protected but fast tank armed with a light anti-tank gun was conceptually similar to the Red Army's own BT series. While these tanks were replaced in production in favour of the T-34 by the summer of 1941, there were plenty of them

Tetrarch tank in a Hamilcar glider, Bovington Tank Museum. The Tetrarch was a tightly-kept secret in order to achieve maximum surprise, which caused a scandal when the Soviet press published a photo of one of these tanks.

still in service in the summer of 1941.[442]

An order was made for the maximum amount on offer, 20 units.[443] These tanks were transferred to the Soviets in Zanjan, Iran, all in one shipment on December 27, 1941.[444] The tanks were a mixed batch. Some of the Tetrarchs were built in late 1940 and already saw service with the 10th Royal Hussars, others were built in the third quarter of 1941 and were brand new. These were some of the first tanks to arrive through the southern route established by the joint Anglo-Soviet invasion of Iran (Operation Countenance) in August-September of 1941. The tanks were delivered through Baku and officially went through the receiving process in January 1942. Due to an absence of instructors and spare parts, the Tetrarchs were only issued to the 21st Independent Training Tank Regiment in March 1942.[445]

An interesting incident took place around this time. The Tetrarch tank was considered a secret by the British. Unlike all other British tanks (barring the Churchill, which was also secret), mentioning it in the Soviet press was forbidden.[446] Nevertheless, a photo of the tank with WD number T.9267 was taken by TASS correspondent Mark Redkin soon after the tanks were issued.[447] These photos were not only published and publicly displayed in the USSR, but also sent to America and published by the Associated Press. A scandal followed, and the images had to be retracted.[448]

Thin armour plates held together by rivets did not offer reliable protection from rifle fire and certain parts could even be broken off with a crowbar. PAVEL BOROVIKOV

Meanwhile, the tanks were moved from the training unit to the 151st Tank Brigade. By June 1942, the brigade was composed of 25 T-26 tanks and 20 Tetrarchs (referred to as MK-7 or MK-VII in documents). The tanks were still a long way from seeing combat. The 151st TBr had an unglamorous task of guarding the border with Turkey to ensure the security of the southern supply route.[449] One of their Tetrarchs was sent to the NIIBT Proving Grounds for trials in July.

A record of the tanks' performance was kept even without combat. Deputy Commander of Repair and Supply of the Transcaucasian Front Engineer-Lieutenant Colonel Galkin wrote a report to the ABTU with his impressions of how well the tanks worked on November 29, 1942. In his words, the tank's engine was powerful, but entirely unsuitable for operation in the cold. Even the relatively mild Caucasian winters required the use of antifreeze.

The tracks also slipped on snow-swept or even wet roads. The driver had to be careful even in good conditions, as many of the tank's components were very weak and cracked or broke as a result of mild shock. Maintenance of the tank was difficult, as many of the controls and transmission elements were unreachable unless the engine was first removed. The tank's roof was thin and also held on so weakly that it could be cracked open with a crowbar.[450]

A similar evaluation was made by the Deputy Commander of the Armoured and Mechanised Forces of the North Caucasian Front, Engineer-Lieutenant Colonel Kalinin. Kalinin judged the tank's top speed to be 60mph (98kph), but rated its average speed on a good road at 30mph (48kph). Like Galkin, Kalinin described the tank as unreliable. The control rods, shock absorbers, and gearbox gears had a very short lifespan.

Kalinin rated the tank's armour poorly,

worse than that of Soviet light tanks. In his evaluation, the tank could be penetrated by mortar shell splinters and the armour could not reliably protect the crew against anything bigger than a submachine gun. Because of the tank's poor reliability and protection, it could only be used on good roads where sharp turns were not required and in situations where the enemy was incapable of offering serious resistance.[451]

The 151st TBr finally received orders to move from its base in Leninakan (modern day Gyumri) on December 30, 1942.[452] The brigade was first attached to the 56th Army, but was reassigned to the 47th Army by January 11, 1943.[453] The tanks first went into battle on January 26. They were sent to attack enemy fortifications in the Kuban known as the Blue Line, a task which neither the 2-pounder gun nor the Tetrarch's thin armour were well suited for.

To the Tetrarch's credit, the T-26 did not fare much better. There were only nine Tetrarchs left in action by the end of the month, collected into one battalion. Four disabled tanks were handed over to the 3rd Rifle Corps to be dug in as fortifications. One returned into service, but five were irreparably lost. The tanks were then passed on to the 132nd ITB, where they did not see combat and only wore themselves down over time. There were only seven Tetrarchs in working order as of May and just two by September.

Six tanks ended up at a repair factory in Tbilisi, half of which were written off and the others repaired some time in 1944. The tanks did not see front line service again and by the summer of 1945 the tank that was sent to the NIBT Proving Grounds for trials was the only one left. Today, it can be seen at the Patriot Park museum.[454]

Cruiser Tanks Mk.IV and Mk.VI

Coincidentally, the history of British cruiser tanks began in the USSR. Lieutenant Colonel Giffard le Quesne Martel observed Soviet exercises held in 1936 and was struck by the speed of the BT tank.[455] The British wanted something similar for their army, and so a number of tanks originally developed as Mediums were reclassified as Cruiser tanks.[456] Bristling with small machine gun turrets and lacking both speed and armour, these tanks were hardly good representatives of the cavalry tank concept.

To develop a Cruiser tank from scratch, the British needed to start at the source. A Christie M.1931 tank was ordered from the United States, which underwent trials under the index A13E1.[457] The Cruiser Tank Mk.III was based on Christie's design, although it lost the ability to drive without tracks. Since the Christie tank arrived with no turret, a new turret similar to the one used on the A9 Medium Tank (reclassified as the Cruiser Tank Mk.I in 1938) was built.

Like the Cruiser Tank Mk.I, the Cruiser Tank Mk.III had just 14mm of armour, enough to make it bulletproof, but not much

Cruiser Tank Mk.III*, Bovington Tank Museum. Although these tanks were roughly equivalent to Soviet BT tanks, the Red Army was fed up with the Liberty engine and its derivatives.

Flames can be seen shooting out of the engine deck of a Centaur tank as its Liberty engine backfires at TankFest 2023. This temperamental engine led to the USSR's rejection of the Centaur tank.

more. This tank was quickly replaced with the Cruiser Tank Mk.IV, a variant with a 30mm armour basis that was also protected from light anti-tank guns.[458]

Even though the Cruiser Mk.IV entered mass production, the War Office was not entirely satisfied with the design. Work began on a Heavy Cruiser, a tank that incorporated satisfactory protection from the very beginning. The work resulted in the A16E1 tank, which ended up too complicated, too heavy, and too expensive.[459]

Designers went back to the A13 programme, putting out two more Cruiser tanks on the Christie chassis: the A13 Mark III (Cruiser Tank Mk.V or Covenanter) and A15 (later known as the Crusader). The latter was better armoured and better armed than its predecessors. The basis for the front armour was 40mm instead of 30, and a secondary machine gun turret was added. A fifth suspension station was added on each side to absorb the extra weight.[460]

The USSR learned about the Cruiser Tank Mk.IV in the fall of 1941.[461] This tank was described as the main Cruiser tank of the British army, capable of independent operation in armoured divisions. However, the USSR showed no interest in these tanks. The Achilles' heel of the British cruisers was their Liberty engine.

The Soviets had plenty of experience with

this model, both with engines purchased abroad and produced inside the USSR under licence as the M-5. These engines proved fire-prone and unreliable in BT series tanks, and the Red Army would not accept any more vehicles with these engines.[462] Additionally, Soviet intelligence obtained a German evaluation of British tanks in North Africa, which was not encouraging.[463] Cruiser Tanks Mk.IV were not ordered.

As shipments of Shermans began to push Crusader tanks out of service with the British army, they were offered to the USSR. Considerable quantities were ready for shipment in early 1943. The British were prepared to send 457 vehicles.[464] Thirty-six could be sent as early as April with convoy JW-55 and 421 more with convoys JW-56 and JW-57 later that year. However, the Liberty engine was once again identified as the Achilles' heel of these designs. GBTU Chief Lieutenant General V. Vershinin diplomatically described the tanks as "modern, but with weak armour", declining the offer on March 11, 1943.[465]

Cruiser Tank Mk. VIII (Cromwell)

The British themselves were not entirely satisfied with the Crusader. The A24 programme launched in November 1940 aimed to replace the Crusader with a heavier cruiser tank. This tank (later indexed Cruiser Tank Mk.VII) would have an armour basis of up to 76mm and a new 57mm 6-pounder gun at an estimated weight of 24 tons, some six tons heavier than the Crusader.[466]

Since the new tank inherited many automotive components including the engine from its predecessor, the reliability was expected to decrease.[467] When British tanks traded numbers for names in 1941, the Cruiser Tank Mk.VII became the Cromwell I.[468]

Another prospective Cruiser Tank project kicked off around this time. The A27 was conceptually similar to the A24, but had a brand new transmission and, more importantly, a new engine. The 600hp Rolls-Royce Meteor derived from the Merlin aircraft engine promised to be much more reliable than the Liberty.

Since production of the new engines still had to rise to meet demand, an intermediate variant was created. The A27L tank was going to be equipped with the

Cromwell IV tank, Patriot Park museum. This is one of six tanks ordered by the USSR for evaluation in 1944. PAVEL BOROVIKOV

QF 75mm Mk.V gun on a Cromwell tank, Vadim Zadorozhniy Technical Museum. This gun gave British tanks an effective HE shell in addition to decent AP performance, but by 1944 it was outclassed both by the T-34-85's ZIS-S-53 gun and the Sherman's 76mm M1A1. PAVEL BOROVIKOV

new transmission and a Liberty engine. The A27M would have the new Meteor engine.

As production of Meteors increased, the A27L could be upgraded to A27M by simply swapping the engine. The A27L tank was called Cromwell II and the A27M was called Cromwell III. These names were changed in August of 1942. The A24 or Cromwell I became the Cavalier I, the A27L or Cromwell II became the Centaur I, and the A27M or Cromwell III became the Cromwell I.[469]

Another important change took place in the fall of 1942. Battlefield experience showed that the Sherman's universal 75mm gun was much more useful than the high velocity 57mm 6-pounder. A decision was made to put the Cromwell into service with the 75mm Vickers QF gun which had the same ballistics as the American 75mm M3.

The USSR was kept up to date on these new vehicles. Two Cromwell I tanks were demonstrated to a Soviet foreign trade representative A. Olkhovsky on November 13, 1942. The tanks performed poorly, suffering from overheating and constant small breakdowns, especially of the suspension springs. The presentation went so badly that Olkhovsky concluded that it must have been staged to reduce Soviet interest in the tank.[470]

The Cromwell's narrow tracks limited its performance in soft soil. PAVEL BOROVIKOV

A Soviet delegation visited a number of British factories that produced Cromwell tanks and their components on March 1, 1943.[471] Puzzlingly, the Soviet observers concluded that the Nuffield Organization alone produced an average of 500 Cromwell family tanks per month.[472] In a letter to Molotov dated April 3, 1943, GBTU Chief Colonel General Fedorenko favourably compared the tank to the Matilda in terms of speed, armour, and armament and asked if this tank could be procured from the British.[473]

The British were not prepared to part with any Cromwells, but offered Centaurs instead. A Centaur tank was shown to a Soviet delegation in May 1943.[474] The tank was swiftly rejected on account of the Liberty engine. The Red Army preferred to take surplus Sherman III (Medium Tank M4A2) tanks instead.[475] The War Office expected the USSR to make another request for Cromwells to follow if the amount of Shermans and Valentines proved insufficient.[476]

The idea of ordering Cromwell tanks resurfaced on March 17, 1944, when the Deputy People's Commissar of Foreign Trade I. F. Semichastnov asked Fedorenko if there was any sense in ordering them now that orders for Valentines were dwindling. By this point, the Red Army was largely capable of supplying its own armoured forces with tanks and a large order was out of the

The running gear proved unreliable during trials. The rubber tyres on the road wheels began to peel off. PAVEL BOROVIKOV

question. Only six vehicles were ordered for evaluation.[477]

These were Cromwell IV tanks, the most common variant of the Cromwell. Cromwell IVs were equipped with 75mm guns and narrow 14.5in tracks. This index was applied to both tanks built as Cromwells as well as Centaurs upgraded with Meteor engines.[478] The six tanks arrived in Baku on August 18, 1944, and made it to the NIBT Proving Grounds by early September. The tank with WD number T.187888 was chosen for brief gunnery and mobility trials, which lasted from September 8 to September 11.[479] The rest of the tanks were used for measurements and study.[480]

The tank showed a high rate of fire. Nine aimed shots per minute could be made when standing still and seven when firing on the move driving at a speed of 9-12kph. It was easy to load the gun from the ready rack, but the loader needed help from other crewmen to reach the shells stowed in other racks.[481] His actions were also constrained by the turret ring, which was considerably narrower than the one on the M4A2 Sherman and T-34-85. The workspace available to the loader was 100mm narrower in both width and depth than on the T-34-85, although the Cromwell's loader enjoyed an extra 100mm of height.[482]

In penetration trials, the QF 75mm Mk.V

Vertical armour held together with rivets and bolts looked downright archaic by 1944. PAVEL BOROVIKOV

gun successfully penetrated the side of a Tiger turret from 500-600m with an M61 shell.[483] This was about the same performance as a Sherman's gun firing the same ammunition[484] and worse than the 6-pounder gun mounted on earlier Cromwells, which penetrated the side of the Tiger from as far as 1,000m.[485] Unlike the loader, the gunner enjoyed a comfortable workspace.[486] He had good visibility and could easily move the gun and look through any of the scopes available to him at the same time.[487]

Only brief driving trials were performed at this stage. The tank drove for 128km alongside a T-34-85 and a Medium Tank M4A2. The T-34-85 was the fastest with a top speed of 55kph, the Cromwell a close second at 52kph, and the M4A2 brought up the rear at 48kph. The British tank maintained a higher average speed: 41 and 26kph on paved and dirt roads respectively. To compare, the T-34-85 achieved an average speed of 35 and 17kph respectively while the M4A2 reached 33 and 20kph. The Cromwell's greater speed came at a cost of fuel economy. The Soviet and American tanks burned 170 and 180L of fuel per 100km of highway driving respectively, while the British burned 280.[488]

Full scale mobility trials began in late September and continued into October. The Cromwell drove for 340km on paved roads, 1,339km on dirt roads, and 152km cross-country. The tank's average speed was 44.7kph, 22.7kph, and 24.3kph respectively. Fuel consumption clocked in at 225, 353, and 370L per 100km. The low speed and high fuel consumption on the dirt road was due to many twists and turns, as well as a generally poor condition of the terrain.

Trials had to end prematurely after 1,823km of driving due to engine trouble. There were other problems. The tracks wore down quickly. Six track links had to be removed by the end of the trials as the tracks stretched out considerably. The tracks were

Exhaust system shroud known as the Normandy Cowl installed on a Cromwell tank, Vadim Zadorozhniy Technical Museum. This shroud was added to deflect exhaust fumes after experience in combat showed that they reveal the tank's location. PAVEL BOROVIKOV

generally found wanting, as they limited the tank's mobility even in areas where it had sufficient engine power to keep driving. The Cromwell's rubber road wheel tyres began to peel off by the end of the run.[489] Performance in swamp trials was also unexceptional. In an 80m long stretch that a T-34-85 could drive through and not sink deeper than 400mm, the Cromwell made it 37.5m before bottoming out. This was slightly better than the M4A2, which could not continue past 33m.[490]

Where the tank lost the most points was the armour. The construction of the tank was downright archaic for 1944. The main armour of the tank was held on by bolts which were attached to a mild steel frame.[491] Soviet specialists were not impressed, as by this point, the USSR had been producing welded tank hulls and turrets for a decade.[492] The vertical placement of armour plates was also criticised as archaic in the Soviet report.[493]

Arrival of information on the use of this tank in Normandy was another blow against the Cromwell. The USSR learned about issues with the exhaust system requiring the installation of the Normandy Cowl, fouling of the spark plugs with oil, and issues with the tearing of the mudflaps. The Meteor engine and auxiliary charger both exhibited issues as well. Design flaws were found in the gun mantlet, emergency escape hatch, idler crank, and tow hooks.[494]

Tank T.187887 remained at the proving grounds and settled at the Kubinka tank museum. Tank T.187866 was disassembled and shot up in the winter of 1944-45. By this time shipments of Medium Tanks M4A2(76)W tanks began to arrive and the small chance of ordering any more Cromwells disappeared entirely. The American tank was better armed and better armoured than the British one. The only advantage the Cromwell had was in speed, but at the cost of much worse fuel efficiency.[495] No additional Cromwells were procured.[496] Upon learning of the A30 Challenger tank in late 1944, the purchase of a sample was discussed, but never made.[497]

This was not a surprising conclusion. Unlike the Sherman or the T-34, the Cromwell could not be fitted with a more powerful gun to keep it competitive on the battlefield. While the Sherman's mobility issues were helped by wider tracks on a HVSS suspension, the wider 15.5in wide tracks used on some marks of the Cromwell did not drastically improve its performance on soft soil. Assembly of the tank with bolts was also a downright old-fashioned solution, although later model tanks eventually received welded hulls with reinforced front armour. These improvements came too late. If the same tank could have been put into action two years prior, it would have been a competitive medium tank. The Cromwell's replacement, the Comet IA, was already in production by the time the USSR began to test it. While the Comet reused some components from the Cromwell, it was largely a new tank.

IV.
Conclusions

It is no secret that American military aid to the USSR during the Second World War eclipsed that of other nations. Colloquially, British aid is lumped under the term 'Lend Lease', even though it had nothing to do with the American programme. American Sherman tanks, American Studebaker trucks, American Airacobra aircraft, and American Willys Jeeps take the centre stage in discussions of foreign aid to the Red Army.

Contributions made by the British are frequently and unjustly sidelined in these discussions. When it comes to tanks, the British were a solid competitor to the Americans. The Red Army received 927 Valentine tanks with 6-pounders, 1,364 Valentines with 2-pounders, and 1,041 Valentine tanks built in Canada (tallied separately in Soviet records) for a total of 3,332 Valentines alone. Deliveries of Valentine tanks outnumbered Shermans until the last year of the war.[498] The delivery of 258 Churchill tanks and 916 Matildas should also not be forgotten.

Soviet records clearly show that these tanks were not accepted out of desperation, as the Red Army was ready and willing to reject any vehicle that did not meet its requirements. British tanks that were deemed fit to serve made their mark in the ranks of the Red Army.

The Churchill was accepted into Guards Heavy Tank Regiments alongside the Soviet KV and IS. Valentine and Matilda tanks played the role of ersatz medium tanks in the most difficult years of the war for the USSR. The Matilda's part began to wane after 1943, but the Valentine remained on the front lines until the campaign against Japan in August of 1945. While accounting for their weaknesses, Red Army reports painted the Matilda, Valentine, and Churchill as useful modern tanks and their crews were decorated for their actions with honours up to and including the title of Hero of the Soviet Union.

Unfortunately for the British tanks, their use peaked in 1942 and early 1943, when the Red Army was fighting brutal positional battles with little success to celebrate. The Matilda and Churchill were outdated by 1944-45 when the Red Army's armoured force truly spread its wings. Even the Valentine gave up the spotlight by that point, despite a second wind granted by the installation of a 6-pounder gun.

Debates rage on regarding the contribution of these tanks to specific battles and how their presence or lack thereof could have turned the tide, but one can confidently say that British assistance had a significant and positive impact on the Soviet-German Front of the Second World War.

This Valentine II tank was one of more than 3,000 Valentine tanks that fought in the Red Army, making it one of the most common foreign tanks to serve under its banner. PAVEL BOROVIKOV

Profiles

Churchill III tank from the 49th Guards Heavy Tank Regiment, Leningrad, January 1943. THIERRY VALLET

Experimental Matilda III tank equipped with a 76mm F-96 gun, December 1941. THIERRY VALLET

Matilda III tank, Battle of Moscow, unknown unit. December 1941. THIERRY VALLET

Matilda III tank, 170th Independent Tank Battalion, 3rd Shock Army, Kalinin Front, January 1943. The plaque on the side reads "Tank of Four Heroes". THIERRY VALLET

Experimental Valentine II tank with a 45mm F-95 gun, December 1941. THIERRY VALLET

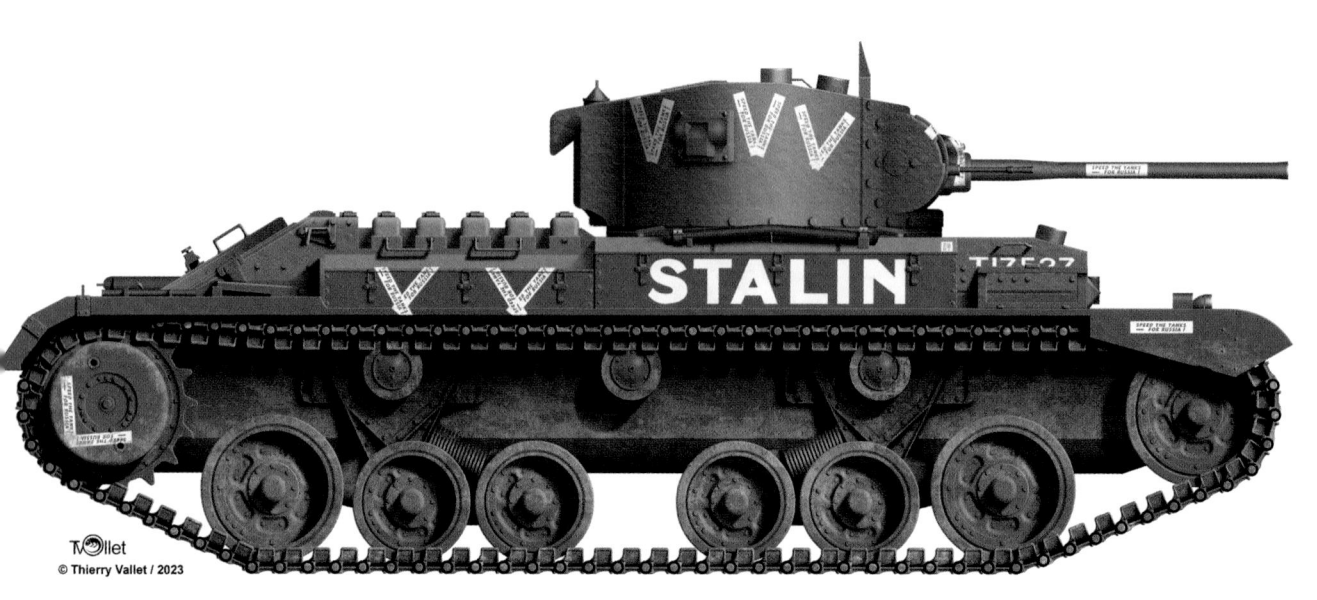

Ceremonial Valentine tank celebrating the shipment of the first British tanks to the USSR. Birmingham Railway Carriage & Wagon Company, September 28, 1941. Thierry Vallet

PROFILES

Canadian-built Valentine VIIA tank, 5th Guards Tank Brigade, North Caucasus Front, summer 1942. THIERRY VALLET

Valentine X tank, 3rd Battalion, 35th Guards Tank Brigade, July 1944. THIERRY VALLET

Glossary

Awards and decorations mentioned in the book in ascending order of prestige:
For Battle Merit medal: awarded for risking one's life in conspicuous and brave actions in defence of the USSR that aided the success of battle.
For Courage medal: awarded for personal courage demonstrated in battle.
Order of the Red Star: awarded for personal courage in battle, excellent performance in a command position, in keeping up battle readiness.
Order of the Patriotic War: awarded for exceptional achievements on the battlefield, in commanding a unit, or for making a significant contribution to the army's battle readiness. Awarded in two classes.
Order of Alexander Nevsky: awarded to commanders of the Red Army that showed personal heroism and exceptional skill in command. This order was generally awarded to commanders of brigades or smaller units.
Order of the Red Banner: awarded for exceptional bravery and courage in dangerous conditions. Initially introduced as the first order of the RSFSR and issued to exceptional commanders in the Russian Civil War, the order remained in use throughout the lifespan of the USSR as one of its highest honours.

Cruiser Tank: A quick and typically lightly armoured tank intended for breakthrough exploitation and long range action.
CS: Close Support. CS tanks were equipped with 3in howitzers that could fire smoke or high explosive shells.
GABTU: *Glavnoye Avto-bronetankovoye Upravleniye*, Main Automobile, Armoured Vehicle, and Tank Directorate. The branch of the military responsible for dealing with design and purchase of military vehicles. Reformed into the **GBTU** (*Glavnoye Brone-Tankovoye Upravleniye*, Main Armour and Tank Directorate) on December 7, 1942.

HK: *Hartkern*. Armour piercing shot with a hard core made of tungsten carbide.
Hl: *Hohlladung*. Shaped charge.
Infantry Tank: A slow moving, heavily armoured tank intended for supporting infantry on the battlefield.
KwK: *Kampfwagenkanone*. Tank gun.
NIBT Proving Grounds: *Nauchno-Issledovatelniy Bronetakoviy Poligon*, Scientific Research Armoured Vehicle Proving Grounds. Located in Kubinka. Presently the site of the Kubinka Tank Museum and Patriot Park.
Pak: *Panzerabwehrkanone*. Anti-tank gun.
Pz: *Panzergranate*. Armour piercing shell.
Sp: *Sprenggranate*. High explosive shell.

Tank units in order of ascending size:
Independent Tank Battalion (ITB): a small tank unit with minimal support assets composed of three tank companies. Independent Tank Battalions were temporarily assigned to accompany rifle regiments in battle.
Guards Heavy Tank Breakthrough Regiment (Gds HTR): a specialised unit composed of 21 heavy tanks. Like independent battalions, these regiments were temporarily attached to rifle divisions or larger tank units to carry out breakthrough missions. Unlike most tank units that earned the title of Guards, heavy tank regiments were formed as Guards units from the start.
Tank Brigade (TBr): a mid-sized tank unit composed of three tank battalions and a motorised infantry battalion. A tank brigade was the smallest tank unit that was expected to operate on its own.
Tank Corps (TC): a large combined arms formation consisting of three Tank and one Mechanised brigades.
Tank Army (TA): a large combined arms formation consisting of several Tank and Mechanised corps.

WD: War Department, the British organisation responsible for army equipment. British tanks were assigned War Department registration numbers prefixed with the letter T.

Endnotes

Introduction

1. Y. Pasholok, *Sovetskiy Pervenets*, https://warspot.ru/11105-sovetskiy-pervenets, retrieved on September 12th, 2023
2. Y. Pasholok, *Ot Teplokhoda AN k MS-1*, https://warspot.ru/11309-ot-teplohoda-an-k-ms-1, retrieved on September 12th, 2023
3. Y. Pasholok, *T-18: Seriynyi Otvet Chemberlenu*, https://warspot.ru/11733-t-18-seriynyy-otvet-chemberlenu, retrieved on September 12th, 2023
4. Y. Pasholok, *Leningradskiy Dvukhbashenniy Yubilar*, https://dzen.ru/media/yuripasholok/leningradskii-dvuhbashennyi-iubiliar-601fe77486f4e22208dca5d3, retrieved on September 12th, 2023
5. Y. Pasholok, *Neudachliviy Pervenets HPZ*, https://dzen.ru/media/yuripasholok/neudachlivyi-pervenec-hpz-5fa129e7a5c3e80d313db772, retrieved on September 12th, 2023
6. TsAMO RF F.31811 Op.1 D.38 L.2-3
7. Y. Pasholok, *Sovetskiy tank-razvedchik s angliyskoy rodoslovnoy*, https://dzen.ru/a/ZETYM1c6b2bSgPfz?sid=108325300911367067, retrieved on September 12th, 2023
8. Y. Pasholok, *Leningradskiy Dvukhbashenniy Yubilar*, https://dzen.ru/media/yuripasholok/leningradskii-dvuhbashennyi-iubiliar-601fe77486f4e22208dca5d3, retrieved on September 12th, 2023
9. P. Samsonov, *Vickers 12 ton in the USSR*, https://www.tankarchives.ca/2013/10/vickers-12-ton-in-ussr.html, retrieved on September 12th, 2023
10. Y. Pasholok, *Pereotsenyonniy Sovietskiy Trekhbashenniy Tank*, https://dzen.ru/media/yuripasholok/pereocenennyi-sovetskii-trehbashennyi-tank-62d3e13b15d67a522f852991, retrieved on September 12th, 2023
11. Canadian Military Headquarters, London (CMHQ), Files Block No. 55–5775 Image 3042
12. Y. Pasholok, *Kolyesno-gusenichniy tupik*, https://warspot.ru/14785-kolyosno-gusenichnyy-tupik, retrieved on September 12th, 2023
13. Y. Pasholok, *Pereotsenyonniy Sovietskiy Trekhbashenniy Tank*, https://dzen.ru/media/yuripasholok/pereocenennyi-sovetskii-trehbashennyi-tank-62d3e13b15d67a522f852991, retrieved on September 12th, 2023
14. Y. Pasholok, *Plavayuschiy tank-razvedchik novogo pokoleniya*, https://dzen.ru/media/yuripasholok/plavaiuscii-tankrazvedchik-novogo-pokoleniia-602bf8c12ca49f594875628a, retrieved on September 12th, 2023
15. P. Samsonov, *War Plans*, https://www.tankarchives.ca/2021/06/war-plans.html, retrieved on September 12th, 2023
16. D. Fletcher, *The Great Tank Scandal*, JJN Publishing, 2021, p.51
17. D. Fletcher, *The Great Tank Scandal*, JJN Publishing, 2021, p.54
18. P. Samsonov, *Matildy i Valentayny na ves zolota*, https://warspot.ru/20687-matildy-i-valentayny-na-ves-zolota, retrieved on September 12th, 2023
19. Ibid

British Infantry Tanks in Soviet Service
Infantry Tank Mk.II (Matilda)

20. Y. Pasholok, *V roli vechno otastayushikh*, https://warspot.ru/18502-v-roli-vechno-otstayuschih, retrieved on September 12th, 2023
21. Y. Pasholok, *Vremennaya koroleva polya boya*, https://warspot.ru/9192-vremennaya-koroleva-polya-boya, retrieved on September 12th, 2023
22. Canadian Military Headquarters, London (1939-1947)–17472, Image 1530-1532
23. Y. Pasholok, *Vremennaya koroleva polya boya*, https://warspot.ru/9192-vremennaya-koroleva-polya-boya, retrieved on September 12th, 2023
24. TsAMO RF F.38 Op.11355 D.298 L.221, 234
25. Y. Pasholok, *Tolstokozhaya ledi na sovetsko-germanskom fronte*, https://warspot.ru/10282-matilda-tolstokozhaya-ledi-na-sovetsko-germanskom-fronte, retrieved on September 12th, 2023
26. Y. Pasholok, *Noviy mech dlya Matildy*, https://warspot.ru/7198-novyy-mech-dlya-matildy, retrieved on September 12th, 2023
27. Y. Pasholok, *Noviy mech dlya Matildy*, https://warspot.ru/7198-novyy-mech-dlya-matildy, retrieved on September 12th, 2023
28. Y. Pasholok, *Tolstokozhaya ledi na sovetsko-germanskom fronte*, https://warspot.ru/10282-matilda-tolstokozhaya-ledi-na-sovetsko-germanskom-fronte, retrieved on September 12th, 2023
29. TsAMO RF F.38 Op.11355 D.1677 L.204
30. TsAMO RF F.38 Op.11355 D.11369 L.21
31. TsAMO RF F.38 Op.11355 D.1677 L.204
32. Y. Pasholok, *Tolstokozhaya ledi na sovetsko-germanskom fronte*, https://warspot.ru/10282-matilda-tolstokozhaya-ledi-na-sovetsko-germanskom-fronte, retrieved on September 12th, 2023
33. TsAMO RF F.38 Op.11380 D.290 L.23-24
34. TsAMO RF F.38 Op.11355 D.290 L.4
35. TsAMO RF F.38 Op.94670 D.23 L.24-25

Infantry Tank Mk.III (Valentine)
The First Generation: Valentine I, Valentine II, Valentine IV

36. Y. Pasholok, *Glavniy tank Lesli Littla*, https://dzen.ru/media/yuripasholok/glavnyi-tank-lesli-littla-619d272c1fa409116dd656d2, retrieved on September 12th, 2023

37. Y. Pasholok, *Pekhotniy optimum,* https://warspot.ru/9495-pehotnyy-optimum, retrieved on September 12th, 2023
38. Y. Pasholok, *Sovetskoye usileniye broni angliyskogo Valentayna,* https://dzen.ru/a/YTJiJHHId2dH_llG, retrieved on September 12th, 2023
39. Canadian Military Headquarters, London (1939-1947)–17472, Image 1530-1532
40. Y. Pasholok, *Pekhotniy optimum,* https://warspot.ru/9495-pehotnyy-optimum,, retrieved on September 12th, 2023
41. Y. Pasholok, *Angliyskaya podderzhka dlya sovetskoy pekhoty,* https://warspot.ru/8287-angliyskaya-podderzhka-dlya-sovetskoy-pehoty, retrieved on September 12th, 2023
42. Y. Pasholok, *Angliyskaya podderzhka dlya sovetskoy pekhoty,* https://warspot.ru/8287-angliyskaya-podderzhka-dlya-sovetskoy-pehoty, retrieved on September 12th, 2023
43. Y. Pasholok, *Pekhotniy anglichanin ne sovsem v svoyey stikhii,* https://dzen.ru/a/YCJ4UgZOyTUYIX9v?sid=67114501269090881, retrieved on September 12th, 2023
44. Y. Pasholok, *Angliyskaya podderzhka dlya sovetskoy pekhoty,* https://warspot.ru/8287-angliyskaya-podderzhka-dlya-sovetskoy-pehoty, retrieved on September 12th, 2023

Return of the Three-Man Turret: Valentine III and V
45. Y. Pasholok, *Bashnya na troikh,* https://warspot.ru/10446-bashnya-na-troih, retrieved on September 12th, 2023
46. Y. Pasholok, *Poderzhanniye Valentinki dlya Krasnoy Armii,* https://dzen.ru/a/X3Qj9Si7RBr9zVJ3?sid=539623425107262666, retrieved on September 12th, 2023
47. Y. Pasholok, *Bashnya na troikh,* https://warspot.ru/10446-bashnya-na-troih, retrieved on September 12th, 2023

Canadian Valentines: Valentine VI, VII, and VIIA
48. P. Samsonov, *Tankisty na golodnom payke,* https://warspot.ru/11523-tankisty-na-golodnom-payke, retrieved on September 13th, 2023
49. Canadian Military Headquarters, London (1939-1947)–17473 Image 603
50. Canadian Military Headquarters, London (1939-1947)–17473 Image 612
51. Canadian Military Headquarters, London (1939-1947)–17473 image 691
52. Canadian Military Headquarters, London (1939-1947)–17473 Image 662
53. Canadian Military Headquarters, London (1939-1947)–17472 Image 1272
54. Canadian Military Headquarters, London (1939-1947)–17472 Image 1350
55. Canadian Military Headquarters, London (1939-1947)–17845 Image 1790
56. Canadian Military Headquarters, London (1939-1947)–17472 Image 1502
57. Canadian Military Headquarters, London (1939-1947)–17472 Image 1511
58. P. Samsonov, *Perviye tanki Kanady,* https://warspot.ru/9654-pervye-tanki-kanady, retrieved on September 13th, 2023
59. Y. Pasholok, *Kanadskiy Valentine,* https://warspot.ru/10088-kanadskiy-valentine, retrieved on September 13th, 2023
60. P. Samsonov, *Perviye tanki Kanady,* https://warspot.ru/9654-pervye-tanki-kanady, retrieved on September 13th, 2023
61. Canadian Military Headquarters, London (1939-1947)–17503 Image 453
62. Canadian Military Headquarters, London (1939-1947)–17503 image 644
63. Canadian Military Headquarters, London (1939-1947)–17866 Image 1016
64. Y. Pasholok, *Kanadskiy Valentine,* https://warspot.ru/10088-kanadskiy-valentine, retrieved on September 13th, 2023
65. Ibid
66. Ibid
67. TsAMO RF F.38 Op.11355 D.754 L.78-88
68. TsAMO RF F.38 Op.11355 D.754 L.78-88
69. Y. Pasholok, *Kanadskiy Valentine,* https://warspot.ru/10088-kanadskiy-valentine, retrieved on September 13th, 2023
70. RF F.38 Op.11355 D.817 L.9-12, 17
71. RF F.38 Op.11355 D.817 L.20-27
72. TsAMO RF F.38 Op.11355 D.817 L.28-34
73. TsAMO RF F.38 Op.11355 D.817 L.35
74. Y. Pasholok, *Kanadskiy Valentine,* https://warspot.ru/10088-kanadskiy-valentine, retrieved on September 13th, 2023
75. P. Samsonov, *Perviye tanki Kanady,* https://warspot.ru/9654-pervye-tanki-kanady, retrieved on September 13th, 2023

Firepower Upgrade: Valentine IX and X
76. Canadian Military Headquarters, London (CMHQ), Files Block No. 55–5775 Image 3073
77. Canadian Military Headquarters, London (1939-1947)–17472 image 982
78. The National Archives, CAB 63/165, *Design and production of heavy tanks* p.88
79. Y. Pasholok, *Otsenka zenitnykh vozmozhnostey,* https://dzen.ru/media/yuripasholok/ocenka-zenitnyh-vozmojnostei-60926135c235fb60b6257b4f, retrieved on September 13th, 2023
80. Y. Pasholok, *Valentin s dlinnoy pushkoy,* https://warspot.ru/10739-valentin-s-dlinnoy-pushkoy, retrieved on September 13th, 2023
81. Y. Pasholok, *Dlinniy stvol dlya pekhotnogo tanka,* https://warspot.ru/11212-dlinnyy-stvol-dlya-pehotnogo-tanka, retrieved on September 13th, 2023
82. Canadian Military Headquarters, London (1939-1947)–17472 Image 880
83. Canadian Military Headquarters, London (1939-1947)–17472 Image 1061
84. Canadian Military Headquarters, London (CMHQ), Files Block No. 55–5788 Image 3417
85. Y. Pasholok, *Valentin s dlinnoy pushkoy,* https://warspot.ru/10739-valentin-s-dlinnoy-pushkoy, retrieved on

86. Y. Pasholok, *Valentin s dlinnoy pushkoy,* https://warspot.ru/10739-valentin-s-dlinnoy-pushkoy, retrieved on September 13th, 2023
87. TsAMO RF F.38 Op.11355 D.1540 L.18-25
88. Y. Pasholok, *Valentin s dlinnoy pushkoy,* https://warspot.ru/10739-valentin-s-dlinnoy-pushkoy, retrieved on September 13th, 2023
89. Canadian Military Headquarters, London (CMHQ), Files Block No. 55–5779 Image 1543-1546
90. Y. Pasholok, *Valentin s dlinnoy pushkoy,* https://warspot.ru/10739-valentin-s-dlinnoy-pushkoy, retrieved on September 13th, 2023
91. Y. Pasholok, *Dlinniy stvol dlya pekhotnogo tanka,* https://warspot.ru/11212-dlinnyy-stvol-dlya-pehotnogo-tanka, retrieved on September 13th, 2023

Soviet Upgrades
92. Y. Pasholok, *Valentin na prokachke,* https://warspot.ru/5305-valentine-na-prokachke, retrieved on September 13th, 2023
93. P. Samsonov, *Local Procurement,* https://www.tankarchives.ca/2020/04/local-procurement.html, retrieved on September 13th, 2023
94. TsAMO RF F.38 Op.11355 D.692 L.203
95. TsAMO RF F.38 Op.11369 D.284 L.62
96. Y. Pasholok, *Pushki pobolshe dlya T-34 ili kak pytatsa v zaytsa zapikhnut utku,* https://dzen.ru/media/yuripasholok/pushki-pobolshe-dlia-t34-ili-kak-pytatsia-v-zaica-zapihnut-utku-5f914951c2b29d2294eca2b0, retrieved on September 13th, 2023
97. Y. Pasholok, *Pekhotniy optimum,* https://warspot.ru/9495-pehotnyy-optimum, retrieved on September 12th, 2023
98. WW2 Equipment Data, *Soviet Explosive Ordnance– 85mm and 100mm Projectiles,* http://ww2data.blogspot.com/2015/09/soviet-explosive-ordnance-85mm-and.html, retrieved on September 13th, 2023
99. Y. Pasholok, *Sovetskiye podkovy dlya angliyskogo Valentayna,* https://dzen.ru/a/Ya2rHQdnsWIidCAA, retrieved on September 13th, 2023
100. TsAMO RF F.38 Op.11355 D.652 L.3-6
101. Y. Pasholok, *Sovetskiye podkovy dlya angliyskogo Valentayna,* https://dzen.ru/a/Ya2rHQdnsWIidCAA, retrieved on September 13th, 2023
102. P. Samsonov, *Sherman Tanks of the Red Army,* Gallantry Books, 2021, p.82
103. M. Baryatinsky, *Tanki lend-liza v boyu,* Yauza, 2009, p.13
104. Y. Pasholok, *Sovetskoye usileniye broni angliyskogo Valentayna,* https://dzen.ru/a/YTJiJHHId2dH_llG, retrieved on September 13th, 2023
105. Y. Pasholok, *Valentin na prokachke,* https://warspot.ru/5305-valentine-na-prokachke, retrieved on September 13th, 2023
106. Y. Pasholok, *Sovetskoye usileniye broni angliyskogo Valentayna,* https://dzen.ru/a/YTJiJHHId2dH_llG, retrieved on September 13th, 2023
107. Y. Pasholok, *Valentin na prokachke,* https://warspot.ru/5305-valentine-na-prokachke, retrieved on September 13th, 2023
108. TsAMO RF F.38 Op.94679 D.22 L.44-45

Infantry Tank Mk.IV (Churchill)
Churchill I – IV
109. D. Fletcher, *The Great Tank Scandal,* JJN Publishing, 2021, p.32
110. D. Fletcher, *The Great Tank Scandal,* JJN Publishing, 2021, p.34
111. The National Archives, CAB 63/165 *Design and production of heavy tanks,* p.54
112. The National Archives, CAB 63/165 Design and production of heavy tanks, p.55
113. D. Fletcher, *The Great Tank Scandal,* JJN Publishing, 2021, p.76
114. D. Fletcher, *The Great Tank Scandal,* JJN Publishing, 2021, p.77
115. The National Archives, CAB 63/165 Design and production of heavy tanks, p.57
116. D. Fletcher, *The Great Tank Scandal,* JJN Publishing, 2021, p.76
117. Canadian Military Headquarters, London (1939-1947)–17885 Image 1877
118. Canadian Military Headquarters, London (1939-1947)–17885 Image 1885
119. The National Archives, CAB 63/165 Design and production of heavy tanks, p.15
120. The National Archives, CAB 63/164 Design and production of heavy tanks, p.11
121. D. Fletcher, *The Great Tank Scandal,* JJN Publishing, 2021, p.77
122. The National Archives, CAB 63/165 Design and production of heavy tanks, p.83
123. The National Archives, CAB 63/165 Design and production of heavy tanks, pp.31-37
124. Canadian Military Headquarters, London (1939-1947)–17472 Image 1530-1532
125. The National Archives, CAB 63/165 Design and production of heavy tanks, p.31
126. Canadian Military Headquarters, London (1939-1947)–17472 Image 1584
127. Canadian Military Headquarters, London (1939-1947)–17472 Image 1648
128. Canadian Military Headquarters, London (1939-1947)–17472 Image 1622
129. Canadian Military Headquarters, London (1939-1947)–17472 Image 1747
130. Canadian Military Headquarters, London (CMHQ), Files Block No. 55–5777 Image 1738
131. Canadian Military Headquarters, London (1939-1947)–17472 Image 1884
132. Canadian Military Headquarters, London (CMHQ), Files Block No. 55–5773 Image 2589
133. Y. Pasholok, *Britanskiy premyer v SSSR,* https://warspot.ru/9660-britanskiy-premier-v-sssr, retrieved on September 14th, 2023
134. The National Archives, FO 954/24B/528, *Soviet Union: General Ismay to Prime Minister Tanks for Russia*
135. TsAMO RF F.38 Op.11355 D.953 L.274-277
136. The National Archives, FO 954/24B/528, *Soviet Union: General Ismay to Prime Minister Tanks for Russia*

137 The National Archives, CAB 63/166, *Design and production of heavy tanks*, p.84
138 Canadian Military Headquarters, London (CMHQ), Files Block No. 55–5788 Image 3417
139 Y. Pasholok, *Britanskiy premyer v SSSR*, https://warspot.ru/9660-britanskiy-premier-v-sssr, retrieved on September 14th, 2023
140 Ibid
141 Ibid
142 M. Baryatinsky, *Tanki lend-liza v boyu*, Yauza, 2009, p.123
143 Y. Pasholok, *Britanskiy premyer v SSSR*, https://warspot.ru/9660-britanskiy-premier-v-sssr, retrieved on September 14th, 2023
144 M. Baryatinsky, *Tanki lend-liza v boyu*, Yauza, 2009, p.122
145 TsAMO RF F.38 Op.11377 D.12 L.18-21
146 Y. Pasholok, *Valentin s dlinnoy pushkoy*, https://warspot.ru/10739-valentin-s-dlinnoy-pushkoy, retrieved on September 13th, 2023
147 M. Baryatinsky, *Tanki lend-liza v boyu*, Yauza, 2009, p.125

Churchill Crocodile
148 Canadian Military Headquarters, London (CMHQ), Files Block No. 55–5776 Image 2322
149 Canadian Military Headquarters, London (CMHQ), Files Block No. 55–5774 Image 1163
150 Canadian Military Headquarters, London (CMHQ), Files Block No. 55–5779 Image 1793-1794
151 Y. Pasholok, *Medlenniy i tolstobronniy*, https://warspot.ru/14829-medlennyy-i-tolstobronnyy, retrieved on September 18th, 2023

Battle of Stalingrad
152 Y. Pasholok, *Britanskiy premyer v SSSR*, https://warspot.ru/9660-britanskiy-premier-v-sssr, retrieved on September 14th, 2023
153 TsAMO RF F.335 Op.5124 D.52 L.105
154 TsAMO RF F.335 Op.5113 D.220 L.9
155 TsAMO RF F.6523 Op.21421s D.9 L.87
156 TsAMO RF F.335 Op.5113 D.234T1 L.178
157 TsAMO RF F.335 Op.5113 D.234T1 L.178
158 TsAMO RF F.335 Op.5113 D.220 L.10
159 TsAMO RF F.335 Op.5113 D.234T1 L.178
160 TsAMO RF F.335 Op.5113 D.234T1 L.178
161 TsAMO RF F.335 Op.5133 D.220 L.12
162 TsAMO RF F.335 Op.5113 D.234T1 L.178
163 TsAMO RF F.335 Op.5124 D.52 L.105
164 TsAMO RF F.33 Op.717037 D.237 L.1-4

Battle of Kursk
165 TsAMO RF F.3403 Op.1 D.18a L.145
166 TsAMO RF F.203 Op.2843 D.438 L.223
167 TsAMO RF F.3403 Op.1 D.7 L.139-140
168 TsAMO RF F.3403 Op.1 D.7 L.139-140
169 TsAMO RF F.3404 Op.1 D.10 L.321
170 TsAMO RF F.3403 Op.1 D.7 L.141
171 TsAMO RF F.3404 Op.1 D.10 L.321
172 TsAMO RF F.3403 Op.1 D.7 L.143-144
173 TsAMO RF F.3415 Op.1 D.17-1 L.7
174 TsAMO RF F.3415 Op.1 D.27 L.115
175 TsAMO RF F.3415 Op.1 D.27 L.116
176 TsAMO RF F.3415 Op.1 D.27 L.117
177 TsAMO RF F.332 Op.4948 D.70 L.159
178 TsAMO RF F.332 Op.4948 D.70 L.162
179 A. Grebnev, *Boyevoye primeneniye tanka Churchill v RKKA*, https://youtu.be/6D_M2KMIf6o?t=3578, retrieved on September 19th, 2023
180 A. Grebnev, *Boyevoye primeneniye tanka Churchill v RKKA*, https://youtu.be/6D_M2KMIf6o?t=3519, retrieved on September 19th, 2023
181 TsAMO RF F.3415 Op.1 D.27 L.100
182 TsAMO RF F.3415 Op.1 D.27 L.102
183 TsAMO RF F.332 Op.4948 D.75 L.49
184 TsAMO RF F.332 Op.4948 D.70 L.203
185 TsAMO RF F.332 Op.4948 D.75 L.103
186 TsAMO RF F.3415 Op.1 D.27 L.119-121
187 TsAMO RF F.332 Op.4948 D.75 L.150
188 TsAMO RF F.332 Op.4948 D.70 L.255
189 TsAMO RF F.332 Op.4948 D.70 L.283
190 TsAMO RF F.332 Op.4948 D.70 L.291
191 TsAMO RF F.332 Op.4948 D.75 L.226
192 TsAMO RF F.332 Op.4948 D.75 L.259
193 TsAMO RF F.332 Op.4948 D.75 L.245
194 TsAMO RF F.3415 Op.1 D.17-1 L.215
195 TsAMO RF F.3415 Op.1 D.27 L.141
196 TsAMO RF F.332 Op.4948 D.71 L.15
197 TsAMO RF F.332 Op.4948 D.76 L.26
198 TsAMO RF F.332 Op.4948 D.76 L.37
199 TsAMO RF F.332 Op.4948 D.76 L.44
200 TsAMO RF F.332 Op.4948 D.76 L.76
201 TsAMO RF F.332 Op.4948 D.76 L.73

Leningrad and Pskov Offensives
202 TsAMO RF F.411 Op.10189 D.1430 L.45
203 TsAMO RF F.217 Op.1221 D.2170 L.64-65
204 TsAMO RF F.217 Op.1221 D.2170 L.70
205 TsAMO RF F.217 Op.1221 D.2170 L.74
206 TsAMO RF F.217 Op.1221 D.2170 L.73
207 TsAMO RF F.411 Op.10189 D.1430 L.45
208 TsAMO RF F.411 Op.10189 D.1430 L.46
209 TsAMO RF F.411 Op.10189 D.1430 L.54
210 TsAMO RF F.411 Op.10189 D.1430 L.58
211 TsAMO RF F.411 Op.10189 D.1430 L.64
212 TsAMO RF F.411 Op.10189 D.1430 L.77
213 TsAMO RF F.411 Op.10189 D.1430 L.80
214 TsAMO RF F.411 Op.10189 D.1191 L.29
215 TsAMO RF F.242 Op.2254 D.179 L.24
216 TsAMO RF F.411 Op.10189 D.1430 L.90
217 TsAMO RF F.411 Op.10189 D.1430 L.93
218 TsAMO RF F.242 Op.2254 D.179 L.14
219 TsAMO RF F.242 Op.2254 D.179 L.18
220 TsAMO RF F.411 Op.10189 D.1430 L.99
221 TsAMO RF F.242 Op.2254 D.179 L.28
222 TsAMO RF F.411 Op.10189 D.1430 L.104
223 TsAMO RF F.1284 Op.1 D.32 L.132
224 TsAMO RF F.242 Op.2254 D.179 L.34
225 TsAMO RF F.411 Op.10189 D.1430 L.107
226 TsAMO RF F.411 Op.10189 D.1430 L.110-111
227 TsAMO RF F.242 Op.2254 D.179 L.44
228 TsAMO RF F.242 Op.2254 D.179 L.50
229 TsAMO RF F.411 Op.10189 D.1430 L.122

230 TsAMO RF F.242 Op.2254 D.179 L.51
231 TsAMO RF F.242 Op.2254 D.179 L.61
232 Tankoviy Front, *36-y gvardeyskiy tyazheliy tankoviy polk proryva*, http://tankfront.ru/ussr/tp/gvtp036t.html, retrieved on September 19th, 2023
233 TsAMO RF F.411 Op.10189 D.1430 L.164
234 TsAMO RF F.411 Op.10189 D.1897 L.12
235 TsAMO RF F.411 Op.10189 D.1430 L.164
236 TsAMO RF F.411 Op.10189 D.1430 L.167
237 TsAMO RF F.411 Op.10189 D.1430 L.174
238 TsAMO RF F.411 Op.10189 D.1430 L.180
239 Tankoviy Front, *36-y gvardeyskiy tyazheliy tankoviy polk proryva*, http://tankfront.ru/ussr/tp/gvtp036t.html, retrieved on September 19th, 2023
240 M. Baryatinsky, *Tanki lend-liza v boyu*, Yauza, 2009, pp. 119-120
241 TsAMO RF F.38 Op.11355 D.290 L.4
242 Y. Pasholok, *Britanskiy premyer v SSSR*, https://warspotru/9660-britanskiy-premier-v-sssr, retrieved on September 14th, 2023
243 The Shadock, *Surviving Infantry tanks Mk IV Churchill (A22)*, http://the.shadock.free.fr/Surviving_Churchills.pdf, retrieved on September 19th, 2023

Matilda and Valentine Tanks in Combat
Battle of Moscow
244 Y. Pasholok, *Pekhotniy anglichanin ne sovsem v svoyey stikhii*, https://dzen.ru/a/YCJ4UgZOyTUYIX9v, retrieved on September 19th, 2023
245 TsAMO RF F.3111 Op.1 D.1 L.3
246 TsAMO RF F.3111 Op.1 D.1 L.7
247 TsAMO RF F.3111 Op.1 D.1 L.4
248 TsAMO RF F.3111 Op.1 D.1 L.5
249 TsAMO RF F.1059 Op.1 D.4a L.48
250 TsAMO RF F.3101 Op.1 D.3 L.31-32
251 TsAMO RF F.3101 Op.1 D.3 L.33-34
252 TsAMO RF F.3101 Op.1 D.3 L.41
253 Y. Pasholok, *Pekhotniy anglichanin ne sovsem v svoyey stikhii*, https://dzen.ru/a/YCJ4UgZOyTUYIX9v, retrieved on September 19th, 2023
254 M. Baryatinsky, *Tanki lend-liza v boyu*, Yauza, 2009, p.87
255 M. Baryatinsky, *Tanki lend-liza v boyu*, Yauza, 2009, pp.103-104
256 TsAMO RF F.3136 Op.1 D.3 L.112
257 TsAMO RF F.3136 Op.1 D.6 L.1(reverse)
258 TsAMO RF F.221 Op.1351 D.176 L.448-449
259 TsAMO RF F.221 Op.1351 D.221 L.26
260 TsAMO RF F.325 Op.4570 D.47 L.22
261 TsAMO RF F.325 Op.4570 D.47 L.27
262 TsAMO RF F.3102 Op.1 D.2 L.8-12
263 TsAMO RF F.3102 Op.1 D.2 L.19
264 TsAMO RF F.3102 Op.1 D.2 L.20-21
265 G.F. Krivosheev and others, *Velikaya Otechestvennaya bez grifa sekretnosti. Kniga poter*, Veche, Moscow, 2009, p.95

Second Battle of Kharkov
266 *Voyenno-politicheskaya obstanovka vesnoy 1942 g.*, http://militera.org/maps/chrono/1900-1949/1942/m24716/, retrieved on September 20th, 2023
267 A. Isayev, *Operatsiya zavershivshayasya katastrofoy*, https://www.youtube.com/watch?v=R_glXXV2-WQ&t=118s, retrieved on September 20th, 2023
268 A. Isayev, *Operatsiya zavershivshayasya katastrofoy*, https://youtu.be/R_glXXV2-WQ?t=480, retrieved on September 20th, 2023
269 A. Isayev, *Operatsiya zavershivshayasya katastrofoy*, https://youtu.be/R_glXXV2-WQ?t=655, retrieved on September 20th, 2023
270 A. Isayev, *Operatsiya zavershivshayasya katastrofoy*, https://youtu.be/R_glXXV2-WQ?t=235, retrieved on September 20th, 2023
271 P. Samsonov, *Deliveries*, https://www.tankarchives.ca/2022/10/deliveries.html, retrieved on September 20th, 2023
272 TsAMO RF F.3443 Op.1 D.6 L.62-63
273 A. Isayev, *Operatsiya zavershivshayasya katastrofoy*, https://youtu.be/R_glXXV2-WQ?t=1160, retrieved on September 20th, 2023
274 TsAMO RF F.3443 Op.1 D.6 L.64
275 TsAMO RF F.3443 Op.1 D.6 L.64
276 TsAMO RF F.229 Op.157 D.14 L.682-683
277 TsAMO RF F.3122 Op.1 D.1 L.8
278 TsAMO RF F.229 Op.157 D.14 L.696
279 TsAMO RF F.229 Op.161 D.881 L.296
280 F.3443 Op.1 D.4 L.43
281 TsAMO RF F.3443 Op.1 D.14 L.1-4
282 TsAMO RF F.3430 Op.1 D.8 L.84
283 TsAMO RF F.3443 Op.1 D.14 L.3
284 TsAMO RF F.1267 Op.1 D.22 L.88
285 TsAMO RF F.3430 Op.1 D.8 L.85
286 TsAMO RF F.3115 Op.1 D.10 L.85
287 TsAMO RF F.3443 Op.1 D.14 L.4
288 TsAMO RF F.3443 Op.1 D.14 L.4
289 TsAMO RF F.3443 Op.1 D.4 L.45-48
290 TsAMO RF F.3443 Op.1 D.4 L.54
291 TsAMO RF F.3233 Op.1. D.7 L.8

Battle of Voronezh
292 TsAMO RF F.3412 Op.1 D.50 L.2
293 TsAMO RF F.3412 Op.1 D.50 L.5
294 TsAMO RF F.331 Op.5041 D.26 L.20
295 TsAMO RF F.331 Op.5041 D.18 L.22
296 TsAMO RF F.331 Op.5041 D.18 L.19
297 TsAMO RF F.331 Op.5041 D.18 L.23
298 TsAMO RF F.331 Op.5041 D.18 L.23
299 TsAMO RF F.331 Op.5041 D.18 L.24
300 TsAMO RF F.331 Op.5041 D.18 L.24
301 TsAMO RF F.3412 Op.1 D.50 L.6
302 TsAMO RF F.331 Op.5041 D.18 L.24
303 TsAMO RF F.3412 Op.1 D.50 L.6
304 TsAMO RF F.331 Op.5041 D.18 L.25-26
305 TsAMO RF F.3412 Op.1 D.50 L.7
306 TsAMO RF F.3412 Op.1 D.50 L.8
307 TsAMO RF F.331 Op.5041 D.18 L.27
308 TsAMO RF F.3412 Op.1 D.50 L.8
309 TsAMO RF F.3412 Op.1 D.50 L.8-9
310 TsAMO RF F.331 Op.5041 D.18 L.32
311 TsAMO RF F.331 Op.5041 D.18 L.35
312 TsAMO RF F.331 Op.5041 D.18 L.38

313 TsAMO RF F.33 Op.682524 D.408 L.22
314 TsAMO RF F.331 Op.5041 D.18 L.41
315 TsAMO RF F.331 Op.5041 D.18 L.40
316 TsAMO RF F.331 Op.5041 D.18 L.46
317 TsAMO RF F.33 Op.682524 D.408 L.14
318 TsAMO RF F.331 Op.5041 D.18 L.50
319 TsAMO RF F.3412 Op.1 D.50 L.19
320 TsAMO RF F.202 Op.5 D.373 L.62-63

Battle of the Caucasus

321 Y. Pasholok, *Tyazhelaya sud'ba lyekogo tanka*, https://warspot.ru/5354-tyazhyolaya-sudba-lyogkogo-tanka, retrieved on September 17th, 2023
322 Y. Pasholok, *Lyogkiye amerikantsy okazavshiyesya v nuzhnoye vremya i v nuzhno meste*, https://dzen.ru/a/Yxu45_H3QTtStwM6, retrieved on September 20th, 2023
323 P. Samsonov, *Local Procurement*, https://www.tankarchives.ca/2020/04/local-procurement.html, retrieved on September 13th, 2023
324 A. Isayev, *Aleksey Isayev o pokhode Gitlera za kavkazskoy neftyu*, https://youtu.be/_a5brHRbNgo?t=472, retrieved on September 20th, 2023
325 M. Baryatinsky, *Tanki lend-liza v boyu*, Yauza, 2009, p.77
326 A. Isayev, *Aleksey Isayev o pokhode Gitlera za kavkazskoy neftyu*, https://youtu.be/_a5brHRbNgo?t=729, retrieved on September 20th, 2023
327 Tankoviy Front, *Upravleniye komanduyushego bronetankhovykh i mekhanizirovannykh voysk Severo-Kavkazskogo fronta*, http://tankfront.ru/ussr/uk-btmv/uk-btmv-f/skf.html, retrieved on September 20th, 2023
328 TsAMO RF F.273 Op.879 D.34 L.12
329 A. Isayev, *Aleksey Isayev o pokhode Gitlera za kavkazskoy neftyu*, https://youtu.be/_a5brHRbNgo?t=563, retrieved on September 20th, 2023
330 TsAMO RF F.273 Op.879 D.35 L.11
331 TsAMO RF F.835 Op.1 D.11 L.7
332 TsAMO RF F.273 Op.879 D.35 L.13
333 Tankoviy Front, *75-y otdelniy tankoviy batalyon*, http://tankfront.ru/ussr/otb/otb075.html, retrieved on September 21st, 2023
334 TsAMO RF F.47 Op.1064 D.2 L.253
335 TsAMO RF F.835 Op.1 D.11 L.9
336 TsAMO RF F.273 Op.879 D.35 L.14
337 TsAMO RF F.47 Op.1064 D.2 L.252
338 TsAMO RF F.835 Op.1 D.11 L.9, TsAMO RF F.273 Op.879 D.35 L.17, TsAMO RF F.47 Op.1064 D.2 L.252
339 Y. Pasholok, *Lyogkiye amerikantsy okazavshiyesya v nuzhnoye vremya i v nuzhno meste*, https://dzen.ru/a/Yxu45_H3QTtStwM6, retrieved on September 20th, 2023
340 TsAMO RF F.47 Op.1063 D.194 L.80
341 TsAMO RF F.273 Op.879 D.35 L.36
342 TsAMO RF F.47 Op.1063 D.194 L.211
343 Y. Pasholok, *Lyogkiye amerikantsy okazavshiyesya vnuzhnoye vremya i v nuzhno meste*, https://dzen.ru/a/Yxu45_H3QTtStwM6, retrieved on September 20th, 2023
344 TsAMO RF F.51 Op.932 D.191 L.1
345 TsAMO RF F.47 Op.1063 D.194 L.52
346 TsAMO RF F.47 Op.1063 D.194 L.129
347 TsAMO RF F.47 Op.1063 D.194 L.140
348 TsAMO RF F.273 Op.879 D.35 L.149
349 Y. Pasholok, *Lyogkiye amerikantsy okazavshiyesya v nuzhnoye vremya i v nuzhno meste*, https://dzen.ru/a/Yxu45_H3QTtStwM6, retrieved on September 20th, 2023
350 TsAMO RF F.51 Op.932 D.133 L.5-6
351 TsAMO RF F.3303 Op.1 D.5 L.22
352 TsAMO RF F.33 Op.682525 D.261 L.20
353 TsAMO RF F.33 Op.682525 D.360 L.31
354 TsAMO RF F.33 Op.682524 D.982 L.8, TsAMO RF F.33 Op.682524 D.982 L.20
355 M. Baryatinsky, *Tanki lend-liza v boyu*, Yauza, 2009, p.79

Battle of Kursk

356 TsAMO RF F.3256 Op.1 D.5 L.2
357 Tankoviy Front, *201-ya tankovaya brigada*, http:/tankfront.ru/ussr/tbr/tbr201.html, retrieved on September 21st, 2023
358 TsAMO RF F.3256 Op.1 D.6 L.124
359 TsAMO RF F.3256 Op.1 D.6 L.168
360 M. Baryatinsky, *Tanki lend-liza v boyu*, Yauza, 2009, p.79
361 TsAMO RF F.3256 Op.1 D.7 L.91
362 TsAMO RF F.3256 Op.1 D.5 L.25
363 TsAMO RF F.3256 Op.1 D.7 L.91-92
364 TsAMO RF F.3256 Op.1 D.7 L.93-95
365 TsAMO RF F.3256 Op.1 D.5 L.33
366 TsAMO RF F.33 Op.682526 D.874 L.72
367 TsAMO RF F.3256 Op.1 D.7 L.95
368 TsAMO RF F.33 Op.682526 D.1731 L.44
369 TsAMO RF F.3256 Op.1 D.7 L.95
370 TsAMO RF F.3256 Op.1 D.7 L.96
371 TsAMO RF F.341 Op.5312 D.285 L.15
372 TsAMO RF F.3256 Op.1 D.7 L.96-97
373 TsAMO RF F.3256 Op.1 D.7 L.99-100
374 TsAMO RF F.3256 Op.1 D.7 L.102
375 TsAMO RF F.33 Op.682526 D.1731 L.13
376 TsAMO RF F.3256 Op.1 D.7 L.104
377 TsAMO RF F.3256 Op.1 D.7 L.107
378 TsAMO RF F.3256 Op.1 D.7 L.111
379 TsAMO RF F.3256 Op.1 D.7 L.112-115
380 TsAMO RF F.3256 Op.1 D.5 L.34
381 TsAMO RF F.3256 Op.1 D.7 L.117
382 TsAMO RF F.3256 Op.1 D.7 L.119
383 TsAMO RF F.3256 Op.1 D.5 L.35
384 TsAMO RF F.3256 Op.1 D.7 L.120
385 TsAMO RF F.3256 Op.1 D.6 L.207
386 TsAMO RF F.3256 Op.1 D.7 L.123
387 TsAMO RF F.3256 Op.1 D.6 L.48
388 TsAMO RF F.3256 Op.1 D.7 L.127-128
389 TsAMO RF F.341 Op.5330 D.31 L.230-232

Operation Bagration

390 TsAMO RF F.332 Op.4948 D.145 L.8
391 TsAMO RF F.3401 Op.1 D.1 L.6
392 TsAMO RF F.241 Op.2593 D.701 L.7
393 TsAMO RF F.241 L.2593 D.701 L.9-11

394 TsAMO RF F.241 L.2593 D.701 L.12-14
395 TsAMO RF F.332 Op.4948 D.291 L.91
396 TsAMO RF F.332 Op.4948 D.141 L.43
397 TsAMO RF F.332 Op.4948 D.141 L.44
398 TsAMO RF F.241 L.2593 D.701 L.20
399 TsAMO RF F.332 Op.4948 D.189 L.14
400 TsAMO RF F.332 Op.4948 D.291 L.92
401 TsAMO RF F.332 Op.4948 D.149 L.60
402 TsAMO RF F.332 Op.4948 D.291 L.92
403 TsAMO RF F.33 Op.690155 D.6861 L.13
404 TsAMO RF F.33 Op.690155 D.6861 L.11
405 TsAMO RF F.33 Op.690155 D.6861 L.27
406 TsAMO RF F.332 Op.4948 D.119 L.12
407 TsAMO RF F.332 Op.4948 D.119 L.14
408 TsAMO RF F.332 Op.4948 D.189 L.17
409 TsAMO RF F.332 Op.4948 D.189 L.18
410 TsAMO RF F.332 Op.4948 D.141 L.66
411 TsAMO RF F.332 Op.4948 D.149 L.66
412 TsAMO RF F.332 Op.4948 D.141 L.83
413 W. Schneider, *Tigers in Combat I*, Stackpole Books, 2004, p. 224
414 TsAMO RF F.332 Op.4948 D.141 L.83
415 TsAMO RF F.332 Op.4948 D.189 L.22
416 TsAMO RF F.332 Op.4948 D.189 L.24
417 W. Schneider, *Tigers in Combat I*, Stackpole Books, 2004, p. 224
418 TsAMO RF F.332 Op.4948 D.189 L.24
419 TsAMO RF F.332 Op.4948 D.149 L.71
420 TsAMO RF F.33 Op.686196 D.2051 L.7
421 TsAMO RF F.332 Op.4948 D.189 L.26
422 TsAMO RF F.332 Op.4948 D.141 L.100
423 TsAMO RF F.241 L.2593 D.701 L.35
424 TsAMO RF F.332 Op.4948 D.119 L.18
425 TsAMO RF F.332 Op.4948 D.119 L.19
426 TsAMO RF F.3401 Op.1 D.1 L.375
427 TsAMO RF F.332 Op.4948 D.149 L.180
428 TsAMO RF F.332 Op.4948 D.142 L.11
429 TsAMO RF F.332 Op.4948 D.142 L.236
430 TsAMO RF F.38 Op.11380 D.290 L.23-24
431 TsAMO RF F.3423 Op.1 D.118 L.54
432 TsAMO RF F.233 Op.2309 D.48 L.254
433 M. Baryatinsky, *Tanki lend-liza v boyu*, Yauza, 2009, pp.95-97

British Light Tanks and Cruisers in the USSR

Light Tank Mk.VII (Tetrarch)
434 TsAMO RF F.38 Op.11355 D.298 L.221
435 D. Fletcher, *The Great Tank Scandal*, JJN Publishing, 2021, p.17
436 Canadian Military Headquarters, London (1939-1947)–17472 Image 1253
437 Canadian Military Headquarters, London (1939-1947)–17472 Image 1530
438 D. Fletcher, *The Great Tank Scandal*, JJN Publishing, 2021, p.61
439 TsAMO RF F.38 Op.11355 D.298 L.208
440 D. Fletcher, *The Great Tank Scandal*, JJN Publishing, 2021, p.62
441 Y. Pasholok, *Tyazhelaya sud'ba lyekogo tanka*, https://warspot.ru/5354-tyazhyolaya-sudba-lyogkogo-tanka, retrieved on September 17th, 2023
442 A. Ulanov, D. Shein, *Poryadok v takhovykh voyskakh*, Veche, 2011, p.60
443 AVP RF F.6 Op.4 D.105 P.11 L.84
444 TsAMO RF F.38 Op.11355 D.648 L.156
445 Y. Pasholok, *Tyazhelaya sud'ba lyekogo tanka*, https://warspot.ru/5354-tyazhyolaya-sudba-lyogkogo-tanka, retrieved on September 17th, 2023
446 P. Samsonov, *Censorship,* http://www.tankarchives.ca/2018/10/censorship.html, retrieved on September 17th, 2023
447 Photo 18518/16, Gosudarstvenniy Tsentralniy Muzey Sovremennoy Istorii Rossii
448 Y. Pasholok, *Priklucheniya skorostnykh anglichan na Severnom Kavkaze,* https://dzen.ru/media/yuripasholok/prikliucheniia-skorostnyh-anglichan-na-severnom-kavkaze-60e42c443f7cf726c3f6e42a, retrieved on September 17th, 2023
449 TsAMO RF F.51 Op.932 D.151 L.1
450 Y. Pasholok, *Tyazhelaya sud'ba lyekogo tanka*, https://warspot.ru/5354-tyazhyolaya-sudba-lyogkogo-tanka, retrieved on September 17th, 2023
451 TsAMO RF F.38 Op.11355 D.1722 L.109
452 TsAMO RF F.47 Op.1063 D.201 L.265
453 TsAMO RF F.51 Op.932 D.151 L.1
454 Y. Pasholok, *Priklucheniya skorostnykh anglichan na Severnom Kavkaze,* https://dzen.ru/media/yuripasholok/prikliucheniia-skorostnyh-anglichan-na-severnom-kavkaze-60e42c443f7cf726c3f6e42a, retrieved on September 17th, 2023

Cruiser Tanks Mk.IV and Mk.VI
455 Y. Pasholok, *Kristi na britanskiy maner*, https://warspot.ru/4822-tank-kristi-na-britanskiy-maner, retrieved on September 17th, 2023
456 D. Fletcher, *The Great Tank Scandal*, JJN Publishing, 2021, p.17-18
457 Y. Pasholok, *Kristi na britanskiy maner*, https://warspot.ru/4822-tank-kristi-na-britanskiy-maner, retrieved on September 17th, 2023
458 D. Fletcher, *The Great Tank Scandal*, JJN Publishing, 2021, p.21
459 D. Fletcher, *The Great Tank Scandal*, JJN Publishing, 2021, p.27
460 D. Fletcher, *Crusader and Covenanter Cruiser Tanks 1939-1945 (Google Play edition)*, Osprey Publishing, 2009, pp.4-14
461 TsAMO RF F.38 Op.11355 D.298 L.221
462 Y. Pasholok, *Angliyskiy diktator v podmoskovnykh polyakh*, https://warspot.ru/5034-angliyskiy-diktator-v-podmoskovnyh-polyah, retrieved on September 17th, 2023
463 TsAMO RF F.38 Op.11355 D.651 L.23
464 Y. Pasholok, *Kvadratniy kreyser v Sovetskom Soyuze*, https://dzen.ru/media/yuripasholok/kvadratnyi-kreiser-v-sovetskom-soiuze-634a506104b9eb7857259040, retrieved on September 17th, 2023
465 Y. Pasholok, *Valentin s dlinnoy pushkoy*, https://warspot.ru/10739-valentin-s-dlinnoy-pushkoy, retrieved on

Cruiser Tank Mk.VIII (Cromwell)

466 Canadian Military Headquarters, London (CMHQ), Files Block No. 55–5772 Image 4548
467 The National Archive, CAB 63/164, *Design and production of heavy tanks*, p.36
468 Canadian Military Headquarters, London (1939-1947)–17472 Image 1530
469 D. Fletcher, *Cromwell Tank Vehicle History and Specification,* The Tank Museum, 2021. pp.i-ix
470 Y. Pasholok, *Angliyskiy diktator v podmoskovnykh polyakh,* https://warspot.ru/5034-angliyskiy-diktator-v-podmoskovnyh-polyah, retrieved on September 17th, 2023
471 TsAMO RF F.38 Op.11355 D.1389 L.84
472 TsAMO RF F.38 Op.11355 D.1389 L.92
473 Y. Pasholok, *Kvadratniy kreyser v Sovetskom Soyuze,* https://dzen.ru/media/yuripasholok/kvadratnyi-kreiser-v-sovetskom-soiuze-634a506104b9eb7857259040, retrieved on September 17th, 2023
474 The National Archives, FO 954/3B/458, *Convoys and Supplies to Russia: From War Cabinet Offices Tanks for Russia*
475 TsAMO RF F.38 Op.11355 D.1389 L.79
476 The National Archives, FO 954/3B/461, *Convoys and Supplies to Russia: From War Cabinet Offices Tanks*
477 Y. Pasholok, *Angliyskiy diktator v podmoskovnykh polyakh,* https://warspot.ru/5034-angliyskiy-diktator-v-podmoskovnyh-polyah, retrieved on September 17th, 2023
478 Canadian Military Headquarters, London (1939-1947)–17866 Image 1118
479 Y. Pasholok, *Angliyskiy diktator v podmoskovnykh polyakh,* https://warspot.ru/5034-angliyskiy-diktator-v-podmoskovnyh-polyah, retrieved on September 17th, 2023
480 Y. Pasholok, *Kvadratniy kreyser v Sovetskom Soyuze,* https://dzen.ru/media/yuripasholok/kvadratnyi-kreiser-v-sovetskom-soiuze-634a506104b9eb7857259040, retrieved on September 17th, 2023
481 Y. Pasholok, *Angliyskiy diktator v podmoskovnykh polyakh,* https://warspot.ru/5034-angliyskiy-diktator-v-podmoskovnyh-polyah, retrieved on September 17th, 2023
482 P. Samsonov, *Ergonomics,* http://www.tankarchives.ca/2013/11/ergonomics.html, retrieved on September 18th, 2023
483 Y. Pasholok, *Angliyskiy diktator v podmoskovnykh polyakh,* https://warspot.ru/5034-angliyskiy-diktator-v-podmoskovnyh-polyah, retrieved on September 17th, 2023
484 TsAMO RF F.38 Op.11377 D.12 L.22-23
485 TsAMO RF F.38 Op.11377 D.12 L.18-21
486 P. Samsonov, *Ergonomics,* http://www.tankarchives.ca/2013/11/ergonomics.html, retrieved on September 18th, 2023
487 Y. Pasholok, *Angliyskiy diktator v podmoskovnykh polyakh,* https://warspot.ru/5034-angliyskiy-diktator-v-podmoskovnyh-polyah, retrieved on September 17th, 2023
488 Y. Pasholok, *Kvadratniy kreyser v Sovetskom Soyuze,* https://dzen.ru/media/yuripasholok/kvadratnyi-kreiser-v-sovetskom-soiuze-634a506104b9eb7857259040, retrieved on September 17th, 2023
489 Y. Pasholok, *Kvadratniy kreyser v Sovetskom Soyuze,* https://dzen.ru/media/yuripasholok/kvadratnyi-kreiser-v-sovetskom-soiuze-634a506104b9eb7857259040, retrieved on September 17th, 2023
490 Ibid
491 P. Samsonov, *Cromwell Armour,* https://www.tankarchives.ca/2017/07/cromwell-armour.html, retrieved on September 18th, 2023
492 Y. Pasholok, *Glavniy sovetskiy predvoyenniy tank,* https://dzen.ru/media/yuripasholok/glavnyi-sovetskii-predvoennyi-tank-620e82bcae55db1a4a04b7e5, retrieved on September 18th, 2023
493 Y. Pasholok, *Angliyskiy diktator v podmoskovnykh polyakh,* https://warspot.ru/5034-angliyskiy-diktator-v-podmoskovnyh-polyah, retrieved on September 17th, 2023
494 TsAMO RF F.38 Op.11355 D.2222 L.74-76
495 Y. Pasholok, *Angliyskiy diktator v podmoskovnykh polyakh,* https://warspot.ru/5034-angliyskiy-diktator-v-podmoskovnyh-polyah, retrieved on September 17th, 2023
496 TsAMO RF F.38 Op.11355 D.3016 L.118
497 TsAMO RF F.38 Op.11355 D.2747 L.2

Conclusions

498 TsAMO RF F.38 Op.11355 D.3016 L.118

Index

1st Moscow Conference (aka Three Power Conference) 12
1st Tank Army (German) 58, 87
10th Royal Hussars 105

AEC A183/A184 13
AEC A189 23
AEC A190 23, 35, 36
Alekseev, Politruk 78
Alymov, Major General 41
Andreevka-Komsomolets, Soviet Union 58
Aranovich, A. G. 43
Arkhangelsk, Soviet Union 12, 15, 16, 50
Armoured Vehicle Directorate of the Transcaucasion Front 41
Army Group Centre 96

Babcock and Wilcox 49
Baku, Soviet Union 28, 32, 33, 44, 84, 87, 105, 114
Bandar Shah, Iran (aka Bandar Torkaman) 84
Barvenkovo Salient, 75
Barysaw, Soviet Union 96, 98, 100
Battle of Kharkov (Second) 75
Battle of Kursk 58, 62, 90, 94
Battle of Moscow 12, 68, 71, 73, 74
Battle of Stalingrad 55, 80
Battle of the Caucasus 84, 85
Bayevo, Soviet Union 64
Bedford Twin Six 46
Belenikhino 58
Beliy Kolodez, Soviet Union 78
Belgorod, Soviet Union 58, 61, 62, 90
Belov, Ye. Ye. 73
Berezina river 98, 100
Birmingham Railway Carriage and Wagon Company (BRC&W) 23, 26
Bobr, Soviet Union 98, 100
Bogdanov, S. 44

Bryansk, Soviet Union 81, 83, 90
Budyonny, Semyon 84
Bykovka, Soviet Union 61, 62

Camp Shilo, Manitoba, Canada 35
Canadian Pacific Rail (CPR) Angus Shops 31, 33
Convoy JW-51B
Convoy JW-52 38
Convoy JW-53 50
Convoy JW-54 27
Convoy JW-55 110
Convoy JW-56 110
Convoy JW-56A 40
Convoy JW-57 110
Convoy JW-66 54
Convoy PQ-1 12, 16, 24
Convoy PQ-2 16, 24
Convoy PQ-3 16, 26
Convoy PQ-6 17
Convoy PQ-7 17
Convoy PQ-11 33
Convoy PQ-13 33
Convoy PQ-15 33, 34
Convoy PQ-16 27, 33
Convoy PQ-17 20, 27, 33, 50
Convoy PQ-18 50
Cox, Captain 50

Department of National Defence 28
Directorate of Mechanisation and Motorisation (UMM) 8
Dnieper river 75
Dolgorukovo, Soviet Union 80
Dolgovka, Soviet Union 64
Dolgoye, Soviet Union 80
Don river 55, 75, 80, 84
Dragunovka, Soviet Union 76
Dyukov 78

Eastern Chinese Railway 8
Elkhotovskiye Vorota, Soviet Union 85, 88
Elswick Works 23, 36

factory #112 (Krasnoye Sormovo) 17
Fedorenko, Lieutenant General 17, 40, 113

Galkin, Engineer Lieutenant Colonel 106
GAU (Main Artillery Directorate) 41
GABTU (aka GBTU – Main Directorate of Armaments) 15, 17, 40, 43
General Motors (GMC) 6004 24, 27, 30, 36
Golosnovka, Soviet Union 80
Gorky Automotive and Armour Centre 16, 71, 80, 90
Gremuchiy, Soviet Union 58
Gremyachiy, Soviet Union 90
Grozny, Soviet Union 84, 85
Gumrak, Soviet Union 55
Gundlach periscope 22, 52

Harland & Wolff 15, 45, 46
Hitler, Adolf 12
Hohlov 41
Home Guard 11

Ilyinovka, Soviet Union 81
Ivanovka, Soviet Union 80, 81

Jones, F. W. 30

Kachalino railway station 55
Kalinichenko, Colonel 83
Kalinin, Engineer-Lieutenant Colonel 106
Karev, Yu. N. 88
Katalkin, S. I. 91
Kazan, Soviet Union 10, 17, 25, 68, 69
Kharkov, Soviet Union 62, 75
Khruschevo, Soviet Union 80, 81
Kizlyar, Soviet Union 87
Klimenko, I. G. 88
Klochkov, M. D. 98
Kobylya Snova river 81
Kondrashev, I. A. 42, 43

Krapivenskiye Dvory, Soviet Union 61
Krasniy Oktyabr, Soviet Union 55
Krivoshey, Major 78
Krupki, Soviet Union 98
Krutoy Log, Soviet Union 90, 91
Kuban, Soviet Union 107
Kubinka, Soviet Union 17
Kubinka tank museum 116

Lekhino, Soviet Union 64
Lend Lease Act (aka Act to Promote the Defense of the United States) 12, 118
Leningrad, Soviet Union 62, 66, 75, 84
Le Quesne Martel, Giffard 108
Leyland E148/E149 14
Leyland E170/E171 14
Liberty engine 109-113
Little, Leslie Francis 22, 23
Lobakov, A. S. 43
Losevo, Soviet Union 98
Luchki, Soviet Union 58, 61
Luga, Soviet Union 62
Lukino, Soviet Union 68

Magdeburg, Germany 44
Maikop, Soviet Union 84
Malaya Psinka, Soviet Union 58
Malgobek, Soviet Union 85, 87, 88
Maslova Pristan, Soviet Union 90
McNoughton, General 30
Meadows MAT 104
Metropolitan Cammell Carriage and Wagon Company (MCCW) 23, 27, 104
Mgle, Soviet Union 100
Mikhailovka, Soviet Union 76, 78
Minsk, Soviet Union 96, 98, 100
Mk.IV periscope 19, 26
Moscow, Soviet Union 8, 12, 44, 68, 71, 73, 75, 84, 96, 98
Mozdok, Soviet Union 85, 87, 88
Mudrovka, Soviet Union 100
Murmansk, Soviet Union 32
Murom, Soviet Union 94

NIBT Proving Grounds 17, 25, 38-42, 107, 114
Naro-Fominsk, Soviet Union 71
Nepokrytaya, Soviet Union 76
Nikiforov, P. N. 100
Normandy, France 116
Novosilskoye, Soviet Union 80
Nuffield Organisation 113

Oder river 100
Olega river 78
Olkhovsky, A. 112
Operation Bagration (aka Belorussian Offensive Operation) 96, 100
Operation Barbarossa 68
Operation Countenance 84, 105
Operation Typhoon 68, 75
Ostashkov, Soviet Union 71
Ostrov, Soviet Union 64, 66

Pakharukov, A. D. 98
Paruli, Soviet Union 98
Pasechnikov, I. A. 98
Patriot Park museum 43, 55, 107
Pentsevo, Soviet Union 92
Peschanoye, Soviet Union 76, 78
Pliev, I. A. 101
Pratt, Brigadier 30
Predmostniy, Soviet Union 87
Prokhorovka, Soviet Union 58
Pskov, Soviet Union 62, 64, 66

Red Army
  1st Mechanised Corps 100
  2nd Guards Tank Army 100
  3rd Guards Tank Brigade 96
  3rd Guards Tank Corps 98, 100
  3rd Rifle Corps 107
  5th Guards Tank Army 58, 61, 96, 98, 100
  5th Guards Tank Brigade 88
  5th Guards Tank Corps 58
  5th Tank Army 80, 81, 83
  5th Independent Tank Brigade 71
  6th Guards Army 57
  6th Guards Motorized Rifle Brigade 58
  7th Guards Army 90, 91
  7th Guards Rifle Division 69
  7th Rifle Corps 64
  8th Army 66
  8th Guards Rifle Brigade 87
  9th Army 87
  9th Guards Rifle Brigade 87
  9th Guards Tank Corps 100
  10th Guards Motorcycle Battalion 96
  10th Guards Rifle Corps 88
  11th Guards Army 96
  11th Guards Rifle Corps 87
  11th Tank Corps 80, 81, 83, 90
  12th Motorized Rifle Brigade 80, 81
  13th Tank Brigade 75, 76, 78, 79
  15th Tank Brigade 88
  16th Army 68
  17th Guards Motorcycle Battalion 100
  18th Guards Tank Brigade 96, 100
  18th Tank Corps 58, 61, 62
  19th Guards Tank Brigade 96, 98, 100
  20th Guards Tank Brigade 58, 71
  21st Guards Tank Brigade 58
  21st Independent Training Tank Regiment 105
  22nd Guards Tank Brigade 58
  22nd Tank Corps 75, 78
  23rd Independent Tank Brigade 73
  24th Guards Cavalry Corps 92
  27th Army (aka 4th Shock Army) 71
  29th Tank Corps 58
  31st Guards Heavy Tank Regiment 66
  33rd Rifle Corps 62
  36th Guards Heavy Tank Breakthrough Regiment 58, 61, 62, 66
  36th Tank Brigade 75, 76, 79
  38th Army 66, 75, 78
  39th Tank Regiment 66
  40th Tank Regiment 64, 66
  42nd Guards Rifle Division 61
  46th Rifle Division 66
  47th Army 107
  47th Guards Heavy Tank Breakthrough

INDEX

Regiment 55
48th Guards Heavy Tank Breakthrough Regiment 55
49th Army 73
50th Guards Heavy Tank Breakthrough Regiment 55
51st Guards Rifle Division 55
52nd Tank Brigade 88
53rd Tank Brigade 80, 81
55th Independent Tank Battalion 68
56th Army 107
57th Motorcycle Battalion 100
58th Cavalry Division 101
59th Tank Brigade 80, 81
60th Rifle Regiment 64
62nd Army 55
62nd Rifle Brigade 87
65th Rifle Division 64
67th Army 62, 64, 66
73rd Guards Rifle Division 90
75th Independent Tank Battalion 87, 88
78th Guards Rifle Division 94
78th Rifle Division 68
81st Rifle Division 76
82nd Tank Regiment 66
108th Rifle Division 68
112th Tank Division 71
124th Rifle Division 76, 78
131st Independent Tank Battalion 71
132nd Independent Tank Battalion 73, 87, 107
133rd Rifle Division 73
133rd Tank Brigade 75, 76, 78, 79
136th Independent Tank Battalion 71
137th Tank Battalion 68
138th Tank Battalion 68, 69
139th Tank Battalion 68
146th Independent Tank Brigade 68
151st Rifle Division 87
151st Tank Brigade 106, 107
159th Rifle Regiment 69
160th Tank Brigade 80, 81
167th Tank Brigade 43
167th Tank Regiment 94

170th Independent Tank Battalion 71
170th Tank Brigade 61
171st Independent Tank Battalion 71
181st Tank Brigade 61
191st Training Tank Brigade 84
194th Training Tank Brigade 55
201st Tank Brigade 90-92
211th Guards Rifle Regiment 90
216th Guards Rifle Regiment 55
219th Howitzer Artillery Regiment 69
222nd Rifle Division 71
226th Rifle Division 75, 78
239th Rifle Division 64
249th Independent Tank Battalion 84, 87, 88
258th Independent Tank Battalion 84, 87, 88
260th Guards Heavy Tank Breakthrough Regiment 66
267th Tank Regiment 101
270th Rifle Division 91, 92
295th Tank Battalion 92
296th Tank Battalion 92
314th Rifle Regiment 66
329th Rifle Division 71
376th Heavy Self Propelled Artillery Regiment 96
389th Rifle Division 87
401st Self Propelled Artillery Regiment 64
417th Rifle Division 87
511th Rifle Regiment 64
563rd Independent Tank Battalion 84, 88
593rd Independent Tank Battalion 41
1308th Rifle Regiment 68
1436th Self Propelled Artillery Regiment 96
1496th Self Propelled Artillery Regiment 96
1529th Heavy Self Propelled Artillery Regiment 90
1536th Heavy Self Propelled Artillery Regiment 66
1669th Anti-tank Artillery Regiment 90
1902nd Self Propelled Artillery

Regiment 66
Redkin, Mark 105
Rokossovsky, Lieutenant General 68
Rolls-Royce Merlin 111
Rolls-Royce Meteor 111, 112, 114, 116
Rostov-on-Don, Soviet Union 75, 84

Sangster, A. G. 47, 48
Semichastnov, I. F. 113
Sergeev, I. I. 68
Serpukhov, Soviet Union 73
Severskiy Donets river 75, 90, 92
Shamshin, Major General 78
Slaveni, Soviet Union 98
Smolyany, Soviet Union 98
Sokolov, Captain 33, 34
Solomino, Soviet Union 92
Spasskoye, Soviet Union 81
Spicer gearbox 24
s.Pz.Abt.505 100
SS *City of Flint* 32
SS *Ocean Freedom* 50
Stalin, Joseph 84
Stalingrad, Soviet Union 43, 55, 80, 84
Stepankovo, Soviet Union 68
Stremutka, Soviet Union 66
Strupen, Soviet Union 100
Struts, I. Ya. 81
Sukhaya Vereyka river 81
Svetitsy, Soviet Union 98

Tabriz, Iran 84
Talachyn, Soviet Union 98
tanks / AFVs
    A1E1 Independent 10
    Archer SPG 41
    Bishop SPG 26
    Carden-Loyd Mk.VI 9
    Char B1 29
    Christie M.1931 108
    Cruiser Tank Mk.I 103, 108
    Cruiser Tank Mk.II 22, 103
    Cruiser Tank Mk.III 108
    Cruiser Tank Mk.IV 29, 103, 109, 110
    Cruiser Tank Mk.V Covenanter 12, 29, 109
    Cruiser Tank Mk.VI Crusader 12, 29
    Cruiser Tank Mk.VII Cavalier aka Cromwell I 111-117
    Cruiser Tank Mk.VII Cromwell II aka Centaur I 112-114
    Cruiser Tank Mk.VIII Cromwell III aka Cromwell I 111-117
    Cruiser Tank Comet IA 117
    Grosstractor 10
    Infantry Tank Mk.I 22, 29
    Infantry Tank Mk.II Matilda (aka Medium Tank A12) 12-20, 24, 26, 40, 41, 50, 67-69, 71, 73, 75, 76, 78, 80, 81, 83, 85, 90-92, 94-96, 102, 113, 118, 119
    Infantry Tank Mk.II Matilda I 14
    Infantry Tank Mk.IIA Matilda II 14
    Infantry Tank Mk.IIA* Matilda III 14, 16-18
    Infantry Tank Mk.IIA* Matilda III CS 14, 17
    Infantry Tank Mk.II Matilda IV 15
    Infantry Tank Mk.II Matilda V 15
    Infantry Tank Mk.III Valentine 12, 18, 19, 21-28, 30-44, 67-69, 71, 73, 75, 76, 78, 84, 85, 88, 90-92, 94-96, 98, 100, 102, 113, 118, 119
    Infantry Tank Mk.III Valentine I 22-24
    Infantry Tank Mk.III* Valentine II 18, 22, 24, 25, 27, 35, 38, 40, 68
    Infantry Tank Mk.III Valentine III 26-28, 36, 38
    Infantry Tank Mk.III Valentine IV 22, 23, 27, 32, 44
    Infantry Tank Mk.III Valentine V 26-28
    Infantry Tank Mk.III Valentine VI 28, 32
    Infantry Tank Mk.III Valentine VII 28, 32-35
    Infantry Tank Mk.III Valentine VIIA 28, 32-34
    Infantry Tank Mk.III Valentine VIII 36
    Infantry Tank Mk.III Valentine IX 36-40, 44, 96, 100

INDEX

Infantry Tank Mk.III Valentine X 36, 40
Infantry Tank Mk.IV Churchill 12, 43, 45-51, 53, 55, 57, 58, 61, 62, 64, 66, 67, 102, 105, 118, 119
Infantry Tank Mk.IVA Churchill II 46, 49-51, 55
Infantry Tank Mk.IV Churchill III 49-51, 55
Infantry Tank Mk.IV Churchill IV 49-51, 53
Infantry Tank Mk.IV Churchill VI 53
Infantry Tank Mk.IV Churchill VII 53, 54
Infantry Tank Mk.IV Churchill VII Crocodile 53-55, 66
IS-2 66, 118
KV-1 11, 17, 19, 51, 55, 66, 71, 74, 80, 81, 83, 88, 118
KV-1S 43, 55, 66
Light Tank M3 84, 85, 87, 88
Light Tank M1917 29
Light Tank Mk.VI 12, 103, 104
Light Tank Mk.VIB 29, 103
Light Tank Mk.VII Tetrarch 12, 103-107
Light Tank Mk.VIII aka Harry Hopkins 104
Mark V heavy tank 7
Medium Tank A6 13
Medium Tank A7 13
Medium Tank M2 29
Medium Tank M3 34, 35
Medium Tank M4A2 Sherman 43, 53, 96, 98, 100, 110, 112-115, 117, 118
Medium Tank Mk.A (Whippet) 7
Medium Tank Mk.B (Hornet) 7
Pz.Kpfw.III 26, 35, 36, 52, 87, 94
Pz.Kpfw.IV 36, 94
Pz.Kpfw.V Panther 94, 98
Pz.Kpfw.VI Tiger Ausf.E 52, 61, 94, 98, 100, 114, 115
Pz.Kpfw.38(t) 34, 35
Renault FT 7
Renault NC-27 8
SOMUA S 35 29
SU-76M 96

SU-85 96
SU-122 90, 92
SU-152 66, 90, 96
T-16 7, 8
T-17 8
T-18 8, 9
T-19 8
T-20 8
T-24 8
T-26 9-11, 75, 78, 84, 85, 106, 107
T-27 9, 10
T-28 10, 11
T-34 17, 19, 26, 41, 58, 61, 68, 71, 74, 75, 78, 88-92, 94-96, 98, 100, 104, 117
T-34-85 100, 114-116
T-35 10
T-37A 9, 11
T-38 11
T-40 11
T48 tank destroyer (aka SU-57) 96
T-46 11
T-60 26, 68, 69, 71, 73, 74-76, 78, 80, 81, 83, 85, 88, 90
T-70 58, 61, 89
Vickers-Carden-Loyd M1931 9
Vickers Mk.E Type A/6-tonner 9
Vickers Medium Tank Mk.II/12-tonner 9
Vickers Medium Tank Mk.III/16-tonner 10
Tashirovo, Soviet Union 71
Tavrovo, Soviet Union 92
Tbilisi, Soviet Union 107
Terek river 84, 87, 88
Ternovaya, Soviet Union 94
Terskaya, Soviet Union 87
Timoshenko, Marshal 75
Tomarovka, Soviet Union 62
Toplinka, Soviet Union 92, 94
Tsipki, Soviet Union 98

Vasilyevka-Prelestnoye, Soviet Union 61
Vauxhall Motors 46, 47
Vershinin, V. 110
Vilnius, Lithuania 44

Vistula river 100
Vladivostok, Soviet Union 51, 84
Volga river 84
Volokolamsk, Soviet Union 68
von Kleist, Paul Ludwig Ewald 87
Voronezh, Soviet Union 80, 90
Voroshilov, K. Ye. 11
Voznesenskaya, Soviet Union 87, 88
Vulcan 18
Vyalikaya Ukhaloda, Soviet Union 100
Vyborg, Soviet Union 66

Westinghouse servo 15
Wilson planetary gearbox 13, 19
Wireless Set No.11 23, 34
Wireless Set No.19 23, 34
Woolwich Arsenal 13
Yablochki, Soviet Union 58
Yakovlevo, Soviet Union 80
Yakubovsky, I. A. 43
Yelizarov, V. K. 92
Yudino, Soviet Union 64

Zakharnikov 43
Zanjan, Iran 105
Zayev, Colonel 88
Zelenograd, Soviet Union 69
Zemlyansk, Soviet Union 80
Zezin, Anatoliy Mikhailovich 42, 43
Zhagulo, Lieutenant Colonel 57
Zubarev, S. I. 81, 83
Zuyevo, Soviet Union 64